MAKE SPACE
FOR LIFE

MAKE SPACE FOR LIFE

HUNDREDS OF IDEAS AND PRACTICAL SOLUTIONS TO DECLUTTER YOUR HOME AND STAY UNCLUTTERED

ANGELLA GILBERT
AND
PETER CROSS

BALBOA.
PRESS
A DIVISION OF HAY HOUSE

Balboa Press books may be ordered through booksellers or by contacting:

Balboa Press
A Division of Hay House
1663 Liberty Drive
Bloomington, IN 47403
www.balboapress.com.au
1-(877) 407-4847

ISBN: 978-1-4525-1120-7 (sc)
ISBN: 978-1-4525-1121-4 (e)

Balboa Press rev. date: 09/24/2013

CONTENTS

PREFACE

ANGELLA'S INTRODUCTION

Decluttering is no longer the buzz word that it was when I began my business almost eight years ago. But what's it all about? Decluttering is not just about our physical environment, it affects our mind and our sense of well being. I found after a decade and a half of living out of a suitcase while on my travels that the necessities of life are few, and the pleasures of a simplified life are many.

Since starting my decluttering and organizing business, I have worked with a wonderful variety of clients. Not just in their living areas but also their wardrobes, home offices and garages.

Believe it or not, I delight in my chosen career. My mission is not only to leave clients with a feeling of achievement and pleasure in what we've accomplished together, but also to make it an enjoyable experience. Yes, I really did say 'enjoyable'. I am not one of those controlling, scary people we see on reality TV who condescendingly insist that the poor client throws out anything which hasn't been used for six months. I like to instead create an atmosphere where clients and I enjoy working together focusing on a desired outcome.

Because I've seen the difference decluttering and organizing makes to clients' lives, I'm eager to reach a wider audience. This book is our effort to delve deeper into the subject of clutter, where it comes from, how it plays out in our lives, and how we can change this dynamic and live more balanced lives.

Many clients have asked me whether my ability to organize and declutter is a matter of genes or can be learned—nature or nurture as my friend and co-author Peter says. I've thought about this and believe it's a mix of both. I'm dedicating this book to my dearly departed Mum, who taught me as a small child the benefits of being neat and tidy. This included not just my bedroom but also my appearance. Of course, I regularly disappointed her by coming home from school shoe-less, with grazed knees, and the odd tear or missing button from my beautiful homemade dress.

My mother spent the first twenty odd years of her married life as a busy farmer's wife. Her skills were many, from running the household with four young children, to doing those things we so admired of women of that period: baking, preserving, knitting, sewing, and nurturing a family. And then there was shearing season when she cooked huge nutritious meals for a dozen shearers. She was extraordinary, and I can't recall seeing her flustered, stressed or demonstrating difficulty balancing these numerous duties. In fact, she had real balance in her life at a time when we didn't even know the term 'life balance'. Mum still made time to entertain lavishly, take us to the city shopping, and one of her favorite pastimes—playing cards.

So I guess my sisters and I learnt by osmosis, and then practiced what we learnt.

Having said this, I believe we can all learn new habits, even if untidiness has been ingrained over decades. I call it 'tapping into your self-interest'. That's not really as esoteric as it sounds. We arrive at a stage when all the 'stuff' in our lives becomes overwhelming. And that's a word clients most often use when we first talk—"I'm completely overwhelmed and don't know where to start". That's when we have to look at how we want to live—do we want to continue with the stress and disorganization, or is it time to get off the bed of nails and create our home to be the haven it can be? Or create an office as a truly efficient and pleasurable workspace?

I've grown used to hearing:

"I'm too embarrassed to have my friends come visit because of the state my house is in."

"I'm sick of being nagged by my husband/wife because the house is so cluttered."

"I am spending hours searching for things, and ending up frustrated and cranky."

"The children's toys are scattered throughout the entire house!"

"I'm risking losing work because I'm so disorganized and not keeping on top of my business."

"I know I'm wasting money on buying things I probably already have but I can't be bothered searching for them amongst all the mess." An example of this one would be the six opened reams of paper I found in one client's home office.

"Help, I need structure in my life and can't seem to create it by myself."

I could go on. We are using this book to show you simple ways to declutter your environment, how to find storage in your home (no matter how small it is), and ultimately to become organized. Believe me, there's joy in a beautifully organized home and workplace. Imagine being able to put your hand on anything instantly; to sit down at the end of the day with a glass of wine or cup of tea with a sigh of contentment. If you are always looking at cluttered surfaces, items scattered over the floor, and laundry in the corner, you're going to feel distracted and stressed.

So do read on my friends. Try on some of the ideas throughout our book. And have fun.

And if you have questions on anything we've written I'd love to hear from you. You can contact me at: <u>angella@gioia.net.nz</u>

PETER'S INTRODUCTION

Angella Gilbert and Mary Poppins have much in common. There are differences of course, Mary Poppins sorts out dysfunctional kids and families while Angella helps homeowners, tenants and business people tame a home or company that isn't working as well as it could.

While Mary Poppins disappears attached to an umbrella once her work has been done, Angella arrives by invitation, performs her magic and will always return to take on other assignments. But what Poppins and Angella share is that both arrive somewhere new to be confronted by chaos and confusion which they quickly replace with order and calm. More importantly families or property dwellers are given a plan and a positive mindset that enables them to function at a higher level once either of these two women moves onto her next assignment.

I should have made a note of the date that Angella first entered my life. She had been contacted by my then wife who wanted our kitchen sorted. It wasn't a mess as such, rather overflowing with stuff; some we used every day mixed in with things that were rarely required. A hardly used bread maker was taking up valuable worktop space and things like the out of favor ice cream machine was getting in the way of other appliances. A pattern emerged that was repeated when Angella returned to take on other tasks; she took a few minutes to size up the problem then swung into action.

In retrospect most of her solutions now seem pretty obvious and left me wondering why I hadn't thought of that solution myself. Other ideas were more inspired. We had dozens of drinking glasses for example all heaped together. She established what the two of us needed then found a new home for the rest along with other dinner party bits and pieces. Things like frying pans were housed in a drawer under the hob and cutlery was separated from cooking implements. Angella got us to remove an expensive cake slicer from the box it came in telling us that we'd never use it if it was packed away out of sight. Examples like these seem pretty feeble but there were so many helpful suggestions. The result of all these little changes was dramatic, the kitchen suddenly seemed a lot larger with a lot more space, yet nothing had been thrown away. We quickly got used to the new order and thereafter it was impossible to remember where anything used to be.

Angella returned, on one occasion to sort out Sabina's wardrobe, her office and hobby equipment. A spare bedroom doubled up becoming a craft room. Clothes were divided into summer and winter collections with things for warm weather put into hibernation during the cooler months and vice versa. Then I got her to come back to wade through the tools in the garage and my tip of an office. I have to admit the garage was a dump, apart from my tools everything that didn't have a home elsewhere was left there.

Over the years I had come to anticipate that it would take me as long to assemble tools required to do something like building a bookcase as it would to actually make the thing. I didn't mind this waste of time as there are considerable comforts in procrastination which will be discussed further in Chapter One. My office wasn't much better. I tidied up from time to time but there was always a pile of paper at the end of these sorties and in no time at all the desk and surrounds would be a mess again. Angella suggested that I got some see through plastic envelopes and grouped current projects together, sorted out the stationary, and suggested ways of archiving everything else.

Sabina and I went our separate ways. Since you ask, she wanted kids, I didn't want to add to the two grown up masterpieces I had a hand in producing earlier. Both of us called on Angella as soon as we moved to new premises. My new lounge was chocker with the contents of the garage which included darkroom equipment, handyman tools, a step ladder and much else. This time there wasn't a garage or even a garden shed. Before you could say supercalifragilisticexpialidocious everything had a new home. My saw, collection of screwdrivers, setsquare and tape measures now live in a kitchen cupboard, an eccentric solution but one that suits me fine.

I first thought of writing about Angella after that initial meeting, but failed to follow it through. Then I discovered another hack had more or less written the article I had written in my head, one that tracked the progress through one of these missions. But a mere magazine article hardly does Angella justice, she is far more than just a declutter merchant as will be revealed in the pages ahead. There will be tips aplenty and a comprehensive run down of what you can do to improve the flow in individual rooms. Even small actions can make your home work for you and make your life a lot easier, freeing you up for the things that you really want to do.

When I tell people that I got Angella in, many assumed that she must be a bossy, control freak who comes along and imposes her own solutions on you. Nothing could be further from the truth, I've no idea what her home is like or even what her taste is apart from what she wears; it's all about helping each client by finding solutions that suit them and that they can live with. TV makeover shows with hectoring hosts have a lot to answer for. Showing others your domestic mess is initially humiliating but these feeling are soon replaced with a profound sense of gratitude when a room's potential is revealed.

If I were to dedicate this book to anyone it would be that couple I stayed with back in the seventies whose working day invariably started with a hunt for the car and front door keys which meant that their anxiety levels were unnecessarily raised for a quarter of an hour until one or other of them found these vital objects. The journey to work took an extra half hour as traffic built up during the morning rush hour. They could have done with Angella for a simple solution like a cup hook strategically placed (for those keys), just as the rest of us need her for bigger and more complex solutions.

Writing a book is a journey into the unknown. This is especially true, as in my case, when you don't know a great deal about the subject matter before you set off. It helps to have a robust road map and a good guide. A map points you in the right direction and a guide is able to identify important landmarks. And in Angella Gilbert I had a brilliant guide. We didn't know each other particularly well at the onset: she hadn't written a book before and I am by inclination a slob so this venture was a leap of faith. But my gut feeling was that we could work together and produce something worthwhile. Others can decide whether we have succeeded but I am happy to report that working with Angella was bliss and exceeded my high hopes.

CHAPTER ONE

THE COMFORTS AND CURSES OF CLUTTER

You rarely read pieces celebrating the virtues of clutter. You'll have difficulty finding something about the rewards of being disorganized or even the advantages of being late. Yet there are reasons for these and other apparent failings.

It might seem perverse to look at the role clutter and disorganization plays in our lives. After all this book sets out to show you how to get your act together by helping you find solutions to problems that are holding you back. We would argue that time spent understanding your reasons for living the way you do is time well spent.

Many of the people who ask for Angella's help do so following some sort of crisis. It may be a sudden realization that the way they now live is giving them grief and they need to change. An untidy disorganized home or workplace is stressful and an uncomfortable place to be. It's not just that you can't find things and waste hours hunting for a misplaced pair of spectacles, wallet or potato peeler, but almost every task takes longer: whether it's putting away plates after washing up or stuffing clean clothes into an overfilled wardrobe. Disorganization and mess can lead to arguments and a culture of shame and blame with other members of the household, and even a loss of respect, self esteem and much else as we will see later.

Clients often tell Angella that they are so ashamed of their messy homes that they never invite friends over. Indeed asking someone like Angella to inspect these bombsites can take a great deal of courage. But there are rationales for how we organize our lives and this chapter explores some of them.

If asked, almost everyone would claim to want to be more organized. Most of us would also own up to tidying the house or flat before the arrival of visitors.

A well organized and tidy home reflects well on its occupant, is good for their self-respect and may even offer the bonus of inducing a little envy in visitors.

Apart from domestic clutter like misplaced underwear or towels, there is also all the paperwork and junk that comes into our homes through the internet as well as the mailbox. For our own sanity most of us would like to be able to clear our email inbox, stay on top of our correspondence and lay our hands on a particular book or CD with minimum fuss. Yet for most of us there is a huge gulf between the way we would like to live, the way we present ourselves to the world, and the way we actually are. We are all different and the problems we face vary between us.

At the end of this chapter you will find space to record your top five reasons for explaining the way you live now as we are keen to help you find solutions to your own rather than other people's problems.

For the moment however here are some explanations that we have discovered that may shed insight on why others have under-performing homes or workplaces. Some of these ideas may resonate with you while the rest may mean nothing. But what is clear is that we are the way we are for good reason. If you are able to understand your own particular motive for the way you are the better able you will be to make positive changes. So in no particular order here are our top reasons for leading a cluttered lifestyle.

#1   Learnt helplessness

There is something comforting about being looked after, of having someone else taking charge and thinking for us. A sense of being nurtured is profoundly satisfying and makes us feel special and cared for. Independence on the other hand goes hand in hand with moving outside our comfort zone and can be lonely and make us feel anxious. Being left to your own devices to live independently can feel like being abandoned.

Human babies are helpless and without a parent's or guardian's help will die. For many parents the role of bringing up a child becomes all consuming. The child or children takes over parents' lives and in time the little ones become a vehicle or vehicles for their own frustrated ambition.

Parenting is a dynamic process, the young have to be supported when they are small and vulnerable, but they also need to be given life skills so that they can thrive on their own. Good parents make themselves redundant, at least of day to day matters, and this can be painful for people who have built their lives around their children to the detriment of everything else. Letting go is made harder by soap opera storylines and media reports that suggests the world is a big bad place full of hidden dangers and evil people gleefully waiting to harm the vulnerable. It therefore shouldn't be a surprise to find people who're unable to let go. The role they have given themselves is so all consuming that other interests have been elbowed out and a vacuum remains.

A tangible example of learnt helplessness is when highly educated students bring home dirty laundry for mum to wash and iron. There are comforts for both sides, mum feels that she is still of use and needed and student feels freed from what they perceive to be a mundane and boring task they feel is beneath them. The long term effect of this sort of exchange is that some young people don't develop practical skills and structures needed to live independently and are forever dependent on others in the know.

#2   Nobody showed me

Angella is often told by clients that they never learnt how to organize their wardrobe/ kitchen/ garage or life. It's something else to blame parents for. Things like this are not on a school curriculum either so teachers and education authorities should shoulder some of the blame as well.

Indeed the list of things one could or should be taught during our formative years is endless. What is certain is that children who come from well run and organized homes where there are logical structures in place have a head start on others who come from a chaotic background. Children learn by example even more than by formal learning.

Angella dedicated this book to her mother who died five years ago. She regarded her mum as a shining example who passed on to her many of the qualities, skills and knowledge she now uses in her work. Did Sylvia Gilbert sit Angella and her sisters down and give them a formal teaching session on household management, cooking or anything else for that matter? I doubt it. But the Gilbert girls learnt that it was possible to multi-task (long before that term was used), run a busy home without getting into a flap, make clothes, cook, and still have a life. They loved coming home from school each day to an afternoon tea of milo and freshly baked biscuits, and were often excited to see a newly sewed dress or two hanging on the door.

While she worked hard and long hours, Sylvia wasn't a martyr. She and Ian loved entertaining, and she also found time to regularly catch up with friends for one of her favorite activities—playing cards.

This might be the most important lesson of them all: running a home defined Sylvia, gave her an important role and opportunities to nurture her young and support her husband and his farm but it would never burn her out or diminish her vibrant personality. And she never thought of these jobs as beneath her and something that ought to be done by someone else.

#3   Territorial advantage

Newspaper and magazine offices are fascinating places. Many if not most are open plan jobs with only people at the top of the pile considered important enough to have their own office. Permanent staffers have their own desks but there is generally more people needing to log on and use a computer than there are places for them to do so. In some offices there are desks allocated for temporary workers like freelancers who do occasional shifts, but there are rarely enough to go round so there is an understanding that anyone is able to use any free desk, which includes the workspace of permanent staffers who are out the office.

Almost without exception, desks of permanent staff are a tip: books, files, and old correspondence is piled up round a computer monitor and only that person knows where anything is. Many will claim that they have a system and can find anything, and up to a point they can or at least can find a missing document faster than anyone else. Every so often there is an avalanche and a mountain of paper dramatically descends to the floor to the amusement of everyone.

But in this environment a cluttered workspace serves a couple of important purposes. Firstly an untidy desk repels unwanted interlopers. Most of us might not like living in a mess but it's worth it if it prevents others invading our space when we are not there. Other people's mess is unbearable and is given a wide berth if at all possible.

So it's the clean and tidy desks that are first taken by casual staff who understandably give the messy ones a miss. And when someone has been working on your desk you often return to find the telephone needs to be un-diverted, the computer has the wrong log in and other petty irritants.

Secondly having an untidy desk sends out a message that its owner is extremely busy and hasn't got time to organize his or her workspace. The logic behind this sort of thinking suggests that if they did have enough time to keep a tidy desk or organize themselves they haven't enough to do. Journalists pride themselves on being able to work in any conditions, knocking out a perfect piece of prose from a war zone, or working in a noisy office with constant interruptions from colleagues and telephones, and they take a perverse pride that they not only work but thrive in conditions that would floor everyone else.

You may be wondering what all this has to do with household management. If a guest stays in a house overnight when the children are away and there are a range of bedrooms to stay in and no spare bedroom, will he or she be offered the bedroom that is spotless or the one that is a tip? Stopping someone using your desk or bedroom when you are not using it is difficult to justify as it makes you appear unreasonable. It's really just a way protecting your turf.

#4   Chaos and creativity go hand in hand

The romantic notion of a starving artist or poet eking out an existence in a damp, cold garret has a strange allure for many especially if a secure position in a bank or insurance office has been sacrificed in the process. If you buy into this one you will believe that your art is so important that anything that takes you away from it, things like cooking food or washing yourself, is time that ought to be spent scribbling, painting or creating sculptures.

The secret hope is that at some future point your work will be discovered by your penniless body and displayed for posterity for future generations who see you for what you are: a genius so far ahead of the game that you couldn't be acknowledged in your own lifetime.

Vincent van Gogh is the role model for this kind of thing. Son of a pastor with an unsuccessful career as a clerk behind him as well as a pair of failed relationships, he moved to Paris in 1886 where he proceeded to throw himself into his art, damaging his mental and physical health in the process. Apparently he shot himself "for the good of all." He only sold one painting in his lifetime but left behind a collection of priceless pictures.

Once again you may be asking yourself what has this to do with living with clutter. The point we are making is that some people liken themselves to a romantic figure like Van Gogh, believing that time and energy spent cleaning and organizing themselves or their homes is better spent on their art and the unimportant role of cleaning and tidying should be left to lesser mortals.

#5   Order equals sterility

The obsession with order, uniformity and tidiness you find in institutions like the armed services, old fashioned hospitals and even some schools can have a detrimental effect on many people who have been subjected to this sort of treatment.

Peter started his working life as a sailor in the British Royal Navy and quickly grew to hate having to fold clothes to the size of a seaman's manual, helping lining up beds in a dormitory so they were in a dead straight line, polishing rubbish bins that were never used for their intended purpose, and all the rest of this mad rubbish.

Either you're brainwashed into this warped way of doing things and spend the rest of your life spit and polishing your shoes, making your home as germ free and sterile as an operating theatre or go the other way and become a slob. Peter became a slob.

There are houses that are so clean and tidy that you can never feel comfortable in them. Ones where you stand up after sitting on the sofa and the host dives over to plump up the cushion you have inadvertently scrunched up. Places where you worry about where you put your shoeless feet as your footprints have marked the shag-pile rug and a used coffee cup has to be washed up the moment the final sip has been drunk. If you have got to this stage you don't need this book. You need therapy.

#6   Mess equals freedom

When we were kids we didn't have to put on smart clothes to play. We put on comfortable functional things and it didn't really matter if we got down and dirty. We were free to explore and during these periods away from parents or other adults there were few expectations to this wonderful freedom.

We could make mud pies, dam streams, climb trees, kick around footballs, or just hang out with our friends. In other words we were free to choose how to spend our time and weren't answerable to anyone.

On the other hand we had to scrub up for school or church and even visits to elderly relatives. For many of us, these formal times were stifling and boring. Sure we also had to dress up for birthday parties and other enjoyable events, but for many a strong link developed between freedom and if not filth, at least not having to make an effort to look our best and be organized.

#7   What about my dreams?

It's tough being a kid these days. You might think that working class Victorian kids had it hard being forced up chimneys, working 14 hour factory shifts in cotton mills or sent down into a dark scary mine, but you'd be wrong. Families are generally smaller than those of our forebears and while the little darlings would seem to have it all, expectations are placed on little Luke or Charlotte like never before. Kids are perhaps societies' biggest investment.

On the sporting front parents attend their kid's soccer, cricket or netball matches and expect them to be winners in return for forking out for all that expensive kit. Once it was an achievement to play in a school orchestra, now little Tarquin or Stephanie is expected to be a soloist or a star of musical theatre productions. Time spent doing household chores could be far better spent preparing for or recovering from training or rehearsals.

Worse is that kids are growing up and learning to worship celebs with no discernible talent and who are famous for just being famous. How do you train yourself for this role? For a start you practice by putting yourself in that exclusive group who are so important that their everyday needs are taken care of by others: in other words getting used to having servants. In the absence of a butler, footman or ladies maids a misguided mum or dad will do. You have to start somewhere.

#8   It's not my job

The world is changing. More and more women are smashing through the glass ceiling and there is some evidence that many high flyers model themselves on workaholics like former British Prime Minister Margaret Thatcher who worked an 18 hour day, seven day week running the UK and bossing around everyone else, and she still found time to make her retired husband a cooked breakfast before he headed out for a round of golf. But Mrs T. was exceptional.

For most, having a high status job usually means divesting themselves of low status, poorly paid and non-valued work such as cleaning and tidying.

#9   Cleaning isn't a career

There is no money in cleaning. Cleaners or domestics the world over are among the worst paid people in the workforce. And then most of them have to go home and clean their own homes for nothing. The work of these people goes unnoticed or more correctly is only noticed if it hasn't been done.

For most office workers little elves could be responsible for empting bins or vacuuming carpets as these jobs for the most part are done when the important people have gone home, or early morning before the office opens. Peter had a part time job in a bank once and loved it. In his case he cleaned while the staff came to the end of their working day and he happily listened in to all the gossip and confidential telephone conversations. The assumption was that cleaners were so thick and unimportant you could say anything while they were in the room as it didn't matter.

The low pay and status of domestics means that the only people prepared to do this thankless and menial work are desperate people from the bottom of the pile, migrants from the developing world and others unable to get more lucrative jobs higher up the food chain.

It could be argued that this attitude to the people who clean for a living affects the way many of us think about cleaning: a job we are too important to do. Indeed cleaning is a job most of us aspire not to do.

#10 Shop till you drop

Shopping is the religion of the 21st century. Shopping malls can be likened to cathedrals where the faithful come to worship what is on offer.

Is it a surprise to realize that most of us have far more clothes, kitchen clobber, fitness equipment and even medication than we need or use? Advertisements which bombard us from morning to night, suggest that this product or that will somehow make our lives complete. The result of this is that more is coming into our homes than goes out and it is not long before the house seems too small for the people living there.

#11 Thrift

Just as we were taught that not eating the contents of a dinner plate somehow deprives a third world child of a square meal, throwing away things we no longer need somehow seems wrong. To dump or even give away the rowing machine that clogs up your garage may also be an admission that its purchase has been an expensive mistake and while it is sitting there getting rusty and dusty there is some small hope that you might find some way of getting a return on this pile of junk.

While it is true that there are some talented recyclers out there who are able to make a coffee table out of an old door, bracelets from dinner forks or a priceless bedspread from 274 scraps of fabric, most of us lack the imagination or skills to see hidden potential in these base materials.

But it doesn't stop us adopting a "better not throw this away in case it comes in handy one day" mindset knowing that the redundant wall bracket or broken ice cream scoop will never ever be used.

We also hang onto items of clothing in case flairs come back in or if we discover a way to shed enough weight to slip into a size eight dress or trousers that fit a sports mad teenager.

#12 Hidden Treasures

TV programs like the BBC's Antiques Roadshow have a lot to answer for. Someone brings along a dusty watercolor that has been rotting away in an attic for decades and the bow tied expert waxes lyrical for the next five minutes.

It turns out this picture Uncle Fred bought for pennies at a Boy Scout jumble sale is a long lost masterpiece by a famous Victorian artist and should earn enough at auction to buy a terrace of houses in a fashionable part of town.

Perhaps an extreme example but this program and others like it fuel the fantasy that in among the junk are priceless treasures that might just reverse our fortunes. It's hardly a surprise then that so many of us are reluctant to throw anything away.

#13 Lucky for some

Peter had a work colleague once who was notoriously disorganized. It was a wonder that he ever made it to work and his high sickness level suggested that his inability to control his wallet prevented him from getting there. His need for alcohol, junk food, porn and cigarettes meant that his wage packet was never enough.

He also had a huge collection of books where when flush with cash he would hide five pound notes between the pages of random tomes. His rationale was that he knew remembering which of these books contained money was impossible so he would need to be really desperate to start the long and painful hunt.

This might be an extreme example but a lot of us are victims of a warped logic that finds solace in our inefficiency.

At one stage Peter lived in two terrace houses that he'd knocked into one. It wasn't long before the second house was as cluttered as the first and almost every day included a hunt to find some missing item which could have been left in any of the four bedrooms, home office, two kitchens, the dining room, one of the two lounges, two bathrooms, two cellars, the conservatory or even the garden shed. Understandably he often didn't find what he was looking for but derived great pleasure by unearthing things he'd been looking for in earlier expeditions.

#14 Getting my act together will change me for the worst

Some highly organized people have a reputation for being difficult and mean with time. You ask to see them and they can fit in a 15 minute window in three weeks time. Every moment and movement is accounted for. Peter had a psychiatrist colleague who he asked to see once and was offered an appointment at six a.m. and arrived early to find his colleague was seeing someone beforehand.

Nothing illustrates this point better than the 1986 film "Clockwise" where John Cleese plays the part of a control freak of a headmaster who gets delayed en route to a conference where he is due to address delegates. The more chaotic and disorganized he becomes the more lovable he seems, rather than the bullying prat that he was at the beginning of the movie.

Questions & Answers

Q **I flog my guts out trying to keep my three bedroom villa clean and tidy but the moment I turn my back my husband and kids turn it into a pigsty. My husband is into carpentry but he never cleans up after he has made something and the boys' bedrooms are littered with coffee mugs and old takeaways. They complain I'm making the place too tidy and don't see why they should all have to change just for me. I can't tell you how many arguments we've had and it seems that George sides with my teenage sons, which is very hurtful.**

A Oh dear. It seems that your home has become a battleground with both sides refusing to budge. We suggest that you put up a white flag, suggest a family meeting and offer a truce.

You could promise to stay out the boys' bedrooms provided they agree to return cups and plates to the kitchen; and that you will not be responsible for cleaning up your husband's workspace. You may not agree with the way they live, but we all need our private space and it might be worth losing these battles if it wins you the war. In return for offering to stay out of these spaces you could ask that areas of the house that everyone uses like the kitchen and the lounge are kept reasonably tidy. Some families find that cleaning rotas work for them. Hopefully they will discover that sharing these chores will make living together a lot easier.

Q **My husband has a collection of guns which he has acquired over twenty years. I hate the amount of time and money he lavishes on them but in every other respect he is the perfect partner. Recently he's been talking about displaying some of them on the lounge wall and this led to a bitter argument. I wish he'd get rid of them but I know that if he did he would resent me for it.**

A   People do have the oddest collections and often reasons for a particular attraction have been lost in time. As you say, trying to part Fred from his guns is likely to be detrimental to your marriage and could cause a serious rift if it hasn't already. What we suggest is a compromise. Why not convert a spare bedroom into a gun museum?

Various rifles and pistols could be displayed on the walls, with others shown off in cabinets, and you could also suggest and help find suitable pictures, photos, and ephemera on the subject. Devoting a part of your home to this collection should not only satisfy Fred but means that when the door of this room is closed everything to do with guns is out of your face.

Q   **Frank was a widower when I met him a couple of years ago. He swept me off my feet and we got married within six months of knowing each other. His first wife died about five years ago. I've now moved in with Frank and have found the whole place has his first wife's fingerprints everywhere. This wasn't a problem at first as we were blind to everything but each other but it is starting to fester and I am worried where this will lead.**

A   Emotions as well as houses get cluttered and often there isn't a straightforward practical solution. Some women would have refused to have moved into what had been another woman's home and insisted on a fresh start somewhere else. But to do this would be to avoid the underlying difficulty that Frank's first wife is still present to some extent and will remain so. Having to share the man you love with someone else, even if that person is dead, is painful and a blow to your pride, especially if during the early days of your courtship he seemed to have got over her. But share you must if your relationship with Frank is to flourish. Get him to talk about his first wife and marriage and if possible try to as it were befriend her, after all were she still with us you would be without a man you clearly adore. As for the house, evolution rather than revolution is called for. Take things slowly and resist the urge to throw out chattels from the first marriage that may be charged with meaning.

Q You are spot on about learnt helplessness. I have to do everything for my partner Rob. His parents split up when he was small and his mum did everything short of wiping his bum. I even have to dial a telephone number for him as this is what his mum did and he claims he's now too old to learn. I do all the housework and cooking, which I didn't mind at first as I wasn't working at the time and he was earning lots of money as he's a talented musician and always performing or recording. I love cooking and didn't mind housework but increasingly resent doing all this now I have a job and I'm the only one doing it. Can you help? Nigel.

A Good partnerships are ones where both parties respect what each person brings to the table. It's a trade off if you like which involves the pooling of skills, energy and money. There is no hard and fast rule to say that both partners should earn money or share household chores but the reality is that for many resentment can build up when only one person is bringing in the dosh or doing all the laundry. Learnt helplessness can only be undone when it is understood and there is a genuine desire to change as it is there for a good reason, even if it undermines your relationship. Put your cards on the table, tell Rob what you are and aren't prepared to do and offer to help him master tasks like using a telephone. If he is really not up for change you should consider moving on.

Conclusion

Before considering the case against clutter and disorganization it is worth spending time reflecting on your own reasons for hanging out against order and efficiency. You can of course record your answers on separate paper to avoid the ridicule of others. We would love to hear from you with these examples and will publish the best examples in future editions of this book so please send them to: info@storiesyoucouldtell.com

1. My home/office/wardrobe/laptop (please delete where applicable) isn't as organized as I'd like for the following reasons:

_____

_____

_____

_____

_____

_____

2. The thing that is most troubling me is:

_____

_____

_____

_____

_____

CHAPTER TWO

CLUTTER—
THE CASE AGAINST

I t may feel that there are overwhelming reasons for sticking with lifelong habits and staying with the devil you know. However a mixture of insight, shrewd planning and a belief in the possibility of improvement can lead to permanent and desirable change.

Myths and Realities

In the last chapter we considered why so many of us clutter up our lives, homes and workspaces. But while many of these reasons may have hidden benefits deep down we know that living with clutter and disorganization is time consuming and wasteful and is something most of us would like to do without.

Before considering reasons for change it's worth dispelling some myths that you may have come to believe.

Myth number 1 I'll need a skip

TV shows like "60 Minute Makeover" where a small army of decorators and a camera crew arrives at a house, redecorate four rooms while some lucky home owner is shopping or at work, reinforces the idea that the only way to transform existing properties is by dumping its current furniture and fittings and replacing them with new tat the show's host and its interior designer are keen to plug.

Whatever you think of these programs, Angella loves them while Peter hates them, most homes can be radically transformed without throwing everything away.

In Angella's experience the only time clients have bought in a skip is when the garage needed a massive clear out, and this has only occurred once. In fact, her clients are surprised by two things: firstly how little they have to throw away, a few garbage bags are usually the full extent; and secondly how little they have to buy. Sometimes she suggests they shop for storage containers to organize paperwork, a container for magazines, out of season clothes and sports gear, and particularly for sorting and organizing items in the pantry, fridge and bathroom vanity unit. And that's it.

Decluttering your home or office isn't about throwing out everything you don't use at least once a week. Rather it's finding a way to ensure that things that you use all the time are easily got at and part of a system that is so logical that you can find them without thinking. It is also about organizing less frequently used items and giving them a home that you can readily recall and quickly retrieve. We will be discussing how you do this in more detail in later chapters.

Myth number 2   A decluttered house is sterile and boring

Well it could be but doesn't have to be. The minimalist fad where occupants only displayed a few objects and hid everything else suits some but only a small minority.

Most of us like to display things that we like or are proud of. The best homes are usually full of character and charm and are often an expression of who we are. We're talking here about knick-knacks, paintings, family photographs and numerous useless objects that are only there because we feel they enhance the feel of the place and are often wonderful reminders of achievements of family members. The photograph on the wall with grown up children dressed in hired for the day mortarboard and academic gown is there to tell every visitor that Sarah or Stephen got a third in media studies.

Myth number 3   Keeping a house decluttered is time consuming

When you go into a decluttered home you may be forgiven for thinking that the host or hostess spends hours keeping the place up to scratch. Every available moment is spent picking up clothes, tidying up, organizing and cleaning.

Actually the opposite is true: it's far easier to keep on top of domestic chores when the place remains tidy and organized. Smart planning can ensure that storage is where you need it so it is as easy to put a hat or coat in a spacious wardrobe rather than the dining room table. Likewise magazines and newspapers will be attracted to a well placed rack instead of the kitchen worktop.

You haven't got to move mountains of books to vacuum the lounge, you can get to your cleaning equipment easily as it's all stored in the same place, and because you're not picking up clothes and assorted school gear from off the furniture, it takes much less time to whip around the housework.

Myth number 4   It will all go back to how it was before

This is a common concern and certainly one felt by Peter before he worked alongside Angella in decluttering the first room she showed him how to sort out. What he learnt was that systematic decluttering was fundamentally different from the tidying up he had done up to that point. There is some overlap but the outcomes are different. Here's how:

Tidying up

Sounds stupid but the object of tidying up is to make somewhere look tidy as quickly and as easily as possible. The best way to do this is by hiding things away and out of sight in the nearest drawer. You might go through a pile of papers and throw out the junk mail, file away paid bills and put books back in bookcases. Surfaces are then swept, wiped or dusted and the room looks transformed.

Nothing wrong with this and it may save your blushes if the village gossip or your mother-in-law is coming round for tea but something like this is purely cosmetic and doesn't help in the long run. Indeed hiding things in drawers makes finding them so much harder when you next need them. For example if batteries needed for bicycle lights and the TV remote control are mixed in with shoe polish, dusters, ball point pens and 101 other objects in one drawer, and there is a random collection of other bric-a-brac in others, the next time you need a small battery may involve a treasure hunt that will take you through these drawers as well as the garage, garden shed and bedroom cabinets. You might just give up and buy some more.

Decluttering

Decluttering is a process which starts by standing back and observing (not judging) how a space is used. On one level, homes and offices are machines for living or working in. Each room serves a number of functions and a declutter expert asks her or himself whether this space is doing the job it is needed for now for the people who are using it. Read this book and you're well on the way to becoming an expert.

Decluttering is then about dividing the wheat from the chaff. Sorting out what you need to use all the time, what you need less frequently, what you don't need but want to hang onto, and what you no longer need and is getting in the way. This is not as straightforward as it may seem as so many of the objects we own have an emotional as well as financial value. Declutter experts learn or are born with an ability to make quick decisions about which category of different objects go into which pile.

Angella says she rarely has to tell a client to actually chuck something out. She's noticed that as they work together the client soon gets into the excitement of the task and often makes their own decision easily and quickly as to what stays and what goes.

The next part of the process is finding a home for groups of objects so that anyone using that space knows where to find what they are looking for easily, and knows where to replace an object after they have used it.

As far as possible the more often something is used the more convenient its home should be. You wouldn't store your everyday coffee mugs in the back of an attic but this might be an ideal spot to put the camping equipment that only has one annual outing. Once the home is decluttered, and systems are put in place it is quite easily maintainable.

Myth number 5 It's impossible to teach kids, and husbands to pick up after themselves

Unless they are rebelling against an overzealous control freak, both kids and husbands usually want to live in orderly homes. They won't necessarily say so, or demonstrate it, but deep down we all want to live in a neat and tidy environment. Kids get to see how much easier it is to find their toys, and have more room for play. Husbands also want a home they can be proud of, whether it's so they can invite friends or colleagues around for a drink, or just to be able to find the television remote.

Angella was asked to sort out her friend Bill's prized tool shed and garage. Bill is a builder and avid fisherman so the tool shed had quickly overflowed into the garage and the floors of both garage and tool shed were scattered with tools, strange looking machinery, and fishing lines and lures sufficient to set up his own fishing shop. Bill had no hope of finding a particular tool or machine without a mammoth search amongst all the rubble.

We will be returning to Bill's shed in Chapter 8 on Garages and Sheds. But needless to say he loved what she did and has pretty much maintained the systems put in place since. Angella also sorted out Peter's garage and he can vouch that time spent on individual DIY jobs reduced dramatically when he didn't have to waste time searching for tools or having to clear junk to make a suitable workspace.

Myth number 6   I'm a 'creative' and have stuff which I couldn't throw out

Angella has worked with artists, and when they sorted out all of their precious paintings, art objects, and resources, and created a home for everything by category, they realized that they didn't have to live in absolute disarray. Indeed the most prolific artists need to be organized so they can work effectively.

Archiving old work frees you up so that you can concentrate on your present projects and not be tyrannized by past achievements. Also having all their resources in one spot enabled these artists to quickly pounce on exactly what they wanted without interrupting the flow of their creative juices.

Myth number 7   It's going cost lots of money and involve loads of work

For some a natural response to living in a cluttered environment is to build more bookcases, erect more shelves and even invest in another garden shed.

Angella has encountered many clients who pay hundreds of dollars a year for a storage facility, and no longer remember what the unit contains. Once something's been stored for a year or more it's pretty clear that you don't need it, and probably won't need it in the future. The scary thing is that the quite high fees for these storage facilities come out of your bank account by automatic payment so after a while you forget about it, and just go on paying.

While it's true that most families have more disposable dosh than a generation ago and own more clothes, tools, kitchen gadgets, mountain bikes and computers, building your way out the problem may only hold back the tide so long.

A root and branch review of the present house contents may liberate more additional space that you currently need and selling on things you no longer need may even leave you better off.

Why have things cluttering up your house when they could be cluttering up someone else's?

Myth number 8 Decluttering will be like housework— soul destroying and boring

If like Peter you have spent hours trying to tidy up a room, never quite finished the job and within days the old chaos has returned you will feel like he did—that time spent doing this task could be spent doing something more worthwhile like card games on the computer or watching the washing machine rotate.

Decluttering on the other hand is a bit like putting up wallpaper or tiling a bathroom: the changes are dramatic and lasting. And you never go back to how things were.

When you know that you are making a lasting improvement you do not resent the time taken.

Realities

Homes are remarkably adaptable places. Peter's brother Tim lives in a house in East Sussex, England that was built between 1370 and 1420. Its infrastructure hasn't changed in the past 600 years but you wonder what the builders of this splendid pile would have made of Tim's state of the art recording studio, everyday use of electricity, telephonic and internet connection with the rest of the world, not to mention on tap water and color scheme. Like Tim the rest of us adapt our homes to suit our particular needs.

One of the pleasures of having a job that takes you into other people's houses is that you get to see how they live. One of the joys of being an insurance salesman, telephone engineer, district nurse, vicar, mobile hairdresser, or even a gigolo, is that you get a chance to see what lurks behind the net curtain or Roman blind that would otherwise be out of bounds.

For those of you without this privileged access it might be worth spelling out some of the main ways individuals use their houses.

A safe haven

Most of us would agree that one of the most important functions of a home is to provide a retreat from the world. It's a place to relax and put your feet up after a hard day's toil.

Until fairly recently it was the one place you could go to get away from tobacco smoke and now it's one of the few inside areas where you are still allowed to light up. The home is also somewhere you can watch what you like on the TV, cook when you want and do any number of other activities without being accountable to council by-laws.

A focus for family life

While some people live on their own, most don't. Most people either live with a partner, a nuclear family, extended family, in student digs, hostels, retirement village, old people's home or any number of other configurations. Most of us have lived in different setups during our lives.

And the majority of these places will include semi public and private areas. Friends and visitors may be welcomed into kitchens and lounges but never get to see the inside of a bedroom or even a workshop.

Somewhere to eat, relax, read for pleasure, listen to music, watch junk TV, fart without embarrassment, make love and sleep

Homes are where you do all the above and more or less everything that you do when you are not earning a crust. JB Priestley spoke about three types of education: education from school, the street and the home, which reminds us that we probably assimilate more while being at home than we ever did in a classroom.

Entertainment

The amount of entertainment a home is used for will vary enormously. At one extreme there are people who never let anyone else cross their threshold while at the other you find people whose doors are always open to entertain a procession of family and friends who drop in uninvited at any time. Peter knows such a family and Pauline Hellier claims that she never knows who is sleeping in her home at any time as friends of her grown up sons are always staying the night without asking her.

Most of us would be uncomfortable with arrangements like these and will restrict informal visiting to a few close friends and ask anyone else by invitation only.

Deep freezers, which so many families now have, means that food is available and meals can be rustled up inside or out without prior warning: a godsend for spontaneous hospitality. And the relative wealth of most middle class professionals means that they can acquire enough glasses, crockery and cutlery to lay on a scaled down formal meal you might expect from the Queen at Windsor Castle or Buckingham Palace.

On the other hand other people understandably restrict the hospitality to nibbles and a few beers in front of the plasma while the All Blacks are being turned over by the Poms.

Home entertainment is important and is perhaps the best way to convert a colleague from work into a personal friend; it provides a way to get to know your children's friends and their parents, neighbors or people you wish to network with.

Somewhere to store stuff

A few years ago someone at a British color supplement had the bright idea of photographing the contents of the houses of random families around the globe. The resulting images highlighted, as if we didn't know, the haves and the have-nots. It was staggering to see how little some people required to eke out a basic living compared to how much others owned and lived with.

Storage and easy access to our belongings is a big issue for many if not most of us in the so called developed world. We tend to accumulate this stuff piecemeal as we can afford it. Most of us lack a storage master plan to work out in advance where each jigsaw puzzle piece fits into the large picture so it is hardly a surprise that houses can soon feel as bloated as Homer Simpson after a night at an 'eat as much as you want' restaurant.

Ideally new acquisitions should be found a home the moment they cross the threshold. If a weed is a plant in the wrong place in a garden, then clutter is a possession that either hasn't got a home or it's something waiting to be put away or removed forever.

Growing things

It's perfectly possible to have a welcoming home that doesn't include living plants or dying cut flowers. However, even people without gardens can compensate by planting flowers or shrubs in window boxes or tubs.

Many find that tending plants provides a balance in their lives and a distraction from the grind of everyday stresses. Certainly plants and flowers add color and softness into a domestic environment making it more relaxing.

A place to house pets

Man has co-existed with other animal species since before recorded history and dogs and cats have been bred to make them human play things for a very long time. It's easy to see why.

Many dogs offer loyalty and companionship, and the need for daily walks gives a real reason for regular exercise; while cats are fascinating in that they are answerable to no-one and stay with you under sufferance or at least until a better offer comes along. Then there is the appeal of songbirds, hamsters, rabbits and tropical fish. Quite what some people get out of owning a pet snake or a pair of goldfish eludes us. But it takes all sorts.

My business workplace/home office

For the first time since the Industrial Revolution the number of people working from home in some sort of paid employment is increasing. While there might not be quite as many working from a home office as had been predicted as technology like PCs and the internet made it possible, more and more of us are working from home at least some of the time. Desktop computers, laptops, printers and the rest of the high tech gear so many of us depend on needs to be confined to a certain area in the house if it isn't to take over our lives even more than it already does.

And even people who continue to work away from home are finding that a dedicated space where domestic admin can be centralized, stationary stored and letters typed is a good thing.

It doesn't make sense to have more than one printer in most households so having one in a semi public place like a home office makes a lot of sense. And now that probably almost every family has a computer, there needs to be a space which the kids can also use to do their homework, and explore the internet.

Where I get to express my individuality and character—an outlet for my creativity

Indeed. We have both seen wonderful examples of homes that have been made into magical places. While having a large budget helps, many people with little money are able to make their homes inviting using flair and creativity while others with seemingly unlimited resources live in houses as welcoming as a midnight graveyard.

Where I create my art—painting, sculpture etc

Having an area dedicated to a hobby (dreadful word) like water color painting, modeling, needlepoint and music making is a good idea. Everything you need is readily available so that you can quickly pick up where you were and you can become productive the moment you enter the room.

Doubling a creative space like this with a home office can be confusing and detract from both activities.

In summary . . .

In a nutshell the case for having a decluttered home can be summed up under the following headings:

- It's time saving—you know where to find things, or at least understand the places where different things are stored.
- You save money—you are not replacing things you've lost.
- There is less stress and frustration—the home seems a calmer place and the family lives more harmoniously.
- Productivity and efficiency increases as it is easier to focus on tasks at hand and there are fewer distractions to throw you off track.
- Your home becomes a pleasure to live in.
- And it becomes an attractive place to invite guests and entertain.

Given the requirements we place upon our homes and the amount of things that we increasingly seem to need to sustain a modern lifestyle it's a wonder that we manage to get so much into a single building. But we do and it is only with robust organizational structures that we can fit it all into the homes we live in.

From now on we will be looking at different rooms or areas of a home and considering ways of getting maximum use from that space while being mindful of other considerations like personal preferences, comfort, safety and budget.

Questions & Answers

Q My wife must have the biggest collection of shoes since Imelda Marcos, former first lady of the Philippines. She could wear a different pair every day for 18 months and still have some over. She works hard and this is her thing so I wouldn't want to stop her but I can't help feeling her footwear is taking over the house and sometimes I feel my stuff is being edged out . . .

A Peter knew a drummer who kept 33 drum kits in his house so a need to accumulate is not gender specific. Most homes are not designed for excesses like these so a customized solution needs to be found. With so many pairs of shoes, storage is only part of the problem. Some sort of filing system is needed so an appropriate pair can be found. Maybe this could be done by color coding different types of shoes and numbering them so that a specific pair can be retrieved instantly. There are lots of different types of shoe stackers around, and you could always check out how local shoe shops store their stock. After all your wife must be keeping them in business.

Q I'm convinced that our house has too much clutter but my partner doesn't want to part with anything. Every time I raise this matter we finish up having a blazing argument and I back down. How can we break this deadlock?

A We wonder whether this problem is quite as intractable as it seems to you. Neither of us is against possessions, rather we are against clutter which isn't the same thing. Possessions can either be stored away so as not to get in the way of everyday things, or can be displayed on high shelves on top of cupboards, in corners and of course on bookshelves. Some couples compromise by having a mixture of busy and bare rooms: in other words, areas of the house that suit the collecting proclivities of your partner and emptier rooms that would seem to be more your taste.

Q I like the idea of having a few plants around but I spend a lot of the time on the road and am away up to a week at a time. I don't want to give my house key to a neighbor asking him or her to water them when I'm away.

A No problem. Just as there's slow release fish food to put in your aquarium when you are away from your tropical fish tank for a fortnight, you can rig up a system that drip feeds your plants. You normally find these systems in garden centers, where you can find systems to be used outside, and those which are appropriate for inside the house. A cheaper but equally impressive solution would be a large cactus, which prefers infrequent watering.

Q During the early years of our marriage the place was easy to keep tidy and clutter free. Then the children came along and we accumulated more and more stuff. My husband's parents died suddenly and we got a lot of their things as well and now it is almost impossible to turn around. We'd love to move somewhere larger but that is out of the question at present. What can we do?

A You raise a number of interesting issues. Firstly it would seem that the organizational structures you had in place worked when you were a young couple but don't anymore, and secondly that you have a lot more chattels than you have space for. Finding homes for domestic equipment is not difficult when you have plenty of space and practically impossible when you haven't. Many families believe that they can solve problems by moving to a larger home only to find that in a year or two the new place is bursting at the seams. In Chapter 9 on Downsizing we look at creative ways of making maximum use of limited space. Some of these suggestions may work well for your situation.

Q I have spent my life having order imposed on me. When I was seven I was sent away to boarding school and later I went into the Army where there was an obsession with neatness. I

take no pride in the mess I live in but I'm blowed if I'm going back to those days.

A   Nor should you. Institutions like your old school and the armed services have their reasons for imposing order on pupils or squaddies. What we are offering here is decluttering solutions that many people find enhances their lives and makes maximum use of what space is available to them. We would argue that designing or at least being able to choose how you live will feel different from having a lifestyle imposed on you. Any system you put in place need only make sense to you and any others who live in your household, and it's therefore tailored to your specific needs rather than something forced on everyone.

Q   **Call me a doubting Thomas but I don't believe that decluttering is a long term solution for me. I always seem to be tidying up and throwing things away at home but in no time at all it's back to normal, junk on every surface and the whole place a mess. The strange thing is that I'm not like this at work where I manage to keep a tidy desk. Am I missing something or should I just resign myself to the inevitable?**

A   It seems to us that you are tidying up rather than decluttering. We can't stress enough the difference between the two processes. Perhaps the reason that you are able to keep your desk tidy at work but can't keep the house in order is that there are places to keep everything you need at work and things are returned there after use. It may be that you need more storage space or to make better use of what you have got, but it seems that a root and branch assessment of the way you live and use your property will pay dividends in the long run. It takes time to establish organizational systems at home and find places to keep everything but it can be done if you take it a room at a time, and specific guidance is given in the following chapters.

Conclusion

You might like to use these exercises as part of your planning process. Use an exercise book if you prefer.

1. Write a statement on how decluttering your home will improve the quality of your life and of those living with you.

_____

_____

_____

_____

_____

2. What myths mentioned in this chapter did you believe before, and how has that changed the way you think?

_____

_____

_____

_____

_____

3. Write down how you see your home and what you love most about it.

_____

_____

_____

_____

_____

_____

CHAPTER THREE

KITCHENS

Kitchens are the heart of the home. Perhaps this is because the kitchen is where we nurture ourselves with food and warmth; it's where family congregate and friends chat to us as we prepare drinks or a meal. And it's probably the most used part of the house.

Kitchens come in all shapes and sizes. At one end there are galley kitchens that are hardly bigger than a short corridor, through to huge jobs big enough to contain a pair of snooker tables, with other sizes in between. Most have fitted units although you still find kitchens with free standing pine dressers, cooking islands and everything a modern cook requires.

The clogged heart of the home

Because kitchens are such busy places and serve so many different purposes, they are rooms Angella is most often asked to declutter. Worktops get clogged with homework, library books and unreturned DVDs, not to mention unpaid bills and junk mail. Disorganized cutlery drawers are filled with kitchen utensils, and storage space groans under pressure to accommodate rice cookers, yoghurt maker, fondue sets and other cooking fads that will never be used again.

It's not unusual to find that a family of four own 27 assorted coffee mugs, enough dinner plates to feed a regiment and five saucepans for each electric ring. In this crowded environment, everyday equipment is elbowed out by things that are rarely or never used. Typically searching for a usable potato peeler can take longer than peeling the spuds.

Think about the functions of most kitchens, such as preparation and cooking of food, storage of provisions, china, cutlery and cooking implements, and often an eating area. Is it any wonder why so many of us become overwhelmed trying to find homes for everything and keeping things organized in such a busy area where there is such a throughput of people and provisions.

While many kitchens have insufficient space, just finding adequate storage is not enough. To get maximum use of your kitchen the numerous objects you find there have to be organized into a system that is easily understood by everyone who uses this area. Once sorted it is likely to remain so, needing only the occasional review to remain fit for purpose.

"I don't know where to start"

Before even beginning to declutter a kitchen Angella will already be aware of any problems a client is facing. They may have spoken of lack of room to move, insufficient storage, or frustration at not being able to find things. However the most common cry is "I don't know where to start". This can mean a kitchen hasn't been sorted out for years, there is no system in place, and perhaps there never was.

Kitchens need logical systems so space is used well and it's easy to find everything. Preparing a meal in a well organized kitchen is far easier and less stressful than in a chaotic one. We could venture further and claim it to be an actual pleasure.

Imagine opening a cupboard and instantly finding an appliance or food item that you need rather than having to rummage around through various cupboards and drawers. How much time would it save you every time you prepared a meal, and imagine over a week or year?

The good news is that any kitchen can be transformed by following Angella's proven method. It requires a clear plan, sufficient time and a leap of faith. These transformations follow a four step process that has been adapted from a logical sequence used in business, medicine and nursing consisting of:

- Assessment
- Planning
- Implementation
- Evaluation

Let's go through them one step at a time.

Assessment

The first thing Angella does on entering a kitchen, or any room she's about to work on for that matter, is to take a good hard look. She stands back and studies the big picture and then homes in on individual components, inspecting the content of various drawers and cupboards.

It's vital to stress that she isn't judging a client, just assessing the way the kitchen is currently used. Angella makes it clear that she prefers clients not to tidy up their kitchen before she visits. It's more useful to see exactly what the problem areas are, how a client is or isn't coping, and how the kitchen is being used. Most people are not systems oriented so they probably don't know how to organize a kitchen to get maximum use of the area with minimal hassle.

Uncomfortable though it may feel, it's important to look at the way that the room is currently being used. What are its strong and weak points? Is it easy or difficult to prepare a meal? Is it a welcoming space for family and friends to enjoy a meal together, and are the storage areas being used efficiently?

By this time Angella will have already established who lives in the house and how it is used. Sometimes a widow, living on her own will use her kitchen to cook a huge Sunday meal for her extended family a few times a month; while other couples mostly eat prepared food requiring minimal equipment.

Kitchens can also be dangerous places. There are red hot surfaces, boiling water and toxic substances which can cause potential harm.

When Angella saw co-author Peter's new flat the first thing that struck her about his kitchen was that he had perched a microwave on top of a fridge freezer that was taller than him. He was reaching up to remove boiling hot meals in flimsy containers, which was clearly a hazard, so she immediately suggested that the microwave was moved to the bench top.

It's also important to anticipate that small children spend time in kitchens, not just in their own homes, but when visiting grandparents and parents' friends, so making your kitchen child proof is worth the effort even if there are no children living there.

Here are a few more questions that immediately arise when assessing the space:

- Are bench tops clear and is there enough space to work on?
- Are kitchen gadgets taking up too much space on bench tops?
- Is there space around the stove and cooking area to place hot dishes when they come out of the oven?
- Are the cupboards and pantry well organized?
- Are the most important items to hand when needed e.g. pot mitts beside the stove?
- Are there things in the kitchen that ought to live elsewhere?
- Are waste containers easy to find and use?

How to assess your kitchen

- Stand at the entrance and slowly scan the entire kitchen area.
- Make a note of things that really annoy you, whether it's clutter on bench tops or difficulty finding or reaching ingredients in the pantry. Also record things like brooms and mops that take up space and get in the way.
- Make a note of how frequently you use individual items. Are often used tools and foodstuffs near to hand or hard to get at?
- Are stirring spoons, tongs, cooking oils and spices stored near to where they will be used?
- Note any chronic frustrations you have got so used to living with that you hardly notice them anymore, such as having to shift items around in your pantry, or cupboards, so you can find things.

Making a plan

A plan consists of solutions to the problems that you have identified during your assessment. In other words everything you've written down that's not working as well as it should. Can that broom or mop be re-housed where it won't be in the way? Are there better ways of storing foodstuffs and china and cutlery?

Implementation

Now you've decided where to start make sure you have an uninterrupted hour or two to do the first area. You'll sabotage yourself if you try to fit this into the half hour before the kids come home from school. If you know you've got free time you'll relax and go at your own pace.

Working in one area at a time will prevent you becoming overwhelmed. We recommend starting somewhere like a pantry which is usually the biggest pain in the neck. Then once that's done, move onto the cupboards, drawers and shelves.

Chunking up the task will prevent you looking at the whole kitchen as one big problem and throwing in the towel before you hit your stride. Ticking off or scrubbing out each task after completion is oddly satisfying. It keeps the momentum going and gives you a sense that everything is falling into place.

Evaluate

As you clear space and reorganize the contents of your kitchen, occasionally stand back and assess what you've done. Sometimes you may have to change where you've put something as it's not as convenient as you hoped and will need to go elsewhere. These may only be minor tweaks and much easier to sort now that the kitchen is organized.

It's important that the new arrangements make sense to you and others using the kitchen. We all have different ways of working in this space and what works for one may not work so well for another.

Practical Steps to Declutter your Kitchen

As you go through this process, think about what you need, and what you don't need or ever use. There are almost always items in a kitchen which we have had tucked away, and maybe now replaced with a newer model. This is the time for a clear out. Commit to creating a clutter free, fabulously workable kitchen. Once you've made this decision discarding things you no longer want or need is liberating and fun.

As you declutter keep a black rubbish bag beside you, in particular when you blitz the pantry as it's common to find foods which have passed their use by dates during this exercise. Angella recently turfed out two bags of expired foods from her pantry, fridge and freezer. Many foods have very limited expiry dates and if they've been tucked at the back of the pantry or fridge they may have gone unnoticed.

Bench tops

These include surfaces beside the oven and elements, alongside sinks, and those located under shelving and cupboards. Whether we are fervent cooks, or just busy parents, we need ample workspace.

Appliances such as toaster, juicer, or food processor, are ideally stored in a cupboard or on a pantry shelf. These items are almost always bulky and take up lots of room on bench tops. Once you've gone through your cupboards and pantry you will probably find an ideal corner for these appliances. And many newer homes have appliance 'garages' which fit these larger items.

If you have a cupboard above or alongside the stove, this is often ideal for oils and spices used in cooking. The nearer things are when you need them the more you'll use them.

It's a good idea to store items like ladles, wooden spoons, large knives, and stirrers in a drawer alongside the stove so you can reach them quickly and it saves you having to cross the kitchen. If you don't have a drawer beside the stove, there are other methods for displaying these utensils, whether hanging them on the wall, or standing them in an attractive container.

Keep cookbooks on an eye-level shelf for easy access. We suggest you sort and cull these too—often we use just a few favorite recipe books while the rest gather dust so you might as well give away the books you never open. After all the ones you don't use are just creating clutter.

Cooking a meal is made up of dozens of small tasks. Once your kitchen is sorted, knowing where to find your tools and having them near to hand when you want them saves hours of wasted time.

Cupboards

When sorting out a cupboard, pull everything out and onto benches or a table. It's the best way to see what's there so what is never used can be culled, and what's left can be sorted.

If you have an older style kitchen with cupboards for china rather than deep drawers which are a feature of newer kitchens, then you need to organize your china, and glassware, so that most used items are at the front making them easier to reach with rarely used items given a home behind. Ideally china and glasses should be stored in eye-level cupboards so you're not continually bending down or reaching up.

Keep glasses in one area, large dinner plates, soup plates and side plates grouped together, and cups, saucers and mugs in another. Make sure you're not reaching over tall items to get to lower ones at the back, for instance stacks of often used side plates behind large dinner plates, otherwise you'll be making extra work for yourself.

Make sure each cupboard has its own designated use, and that contents are logically placed (see Emily's case study further on where china was eventually placed on the kitchen side of the servery for use in the dining room).

Lower cupboards such as ones under a sink bench can be used for appliances, and infrequently used pots and pans. Cupboards located under the sink unit are ideal to tuck away the many 'non-toxic' cleaning products, cloths and sponges. Given the hazardous nature of some of these products you might want to store these somewhere higher and therefore safer from exploring hands of small children. Or you can get a kiddie-lock put on the cupboard when the children come to visit.

If there's space in the cupboards under the sink, this area can also be used to store the rubbish and recycling bins. It's useful to have bins handy to where you would scrape food scraps from plates when washing up.

Drawers

If you have deep drawers for pots and pans, plates and dishes, organize them so their location is closest to where you use them. Place pots and pans near the oven and elements; plates and dishes closest to the serving area.

Here are some suggestions on how drawers can be efficiently used:

- Deeper drawers are appropriate for pots and pans, and china.
- Shallow drawers can be used for herbs and spices, and even special teas and coffees.

- Cutlery drawers do need dividers for knives, forks and spoons, and preferably a separate divider for large carving knives and other sharp objects. This should be the top drawer as they are used most frequently.
- Generally, the next drawer down would contain larger implements like soup ladles, stirring spoons, and hand whisks that are used less often, although these items may also be stored as suggested earlier beside the stove.
- Therefore, the second or third drawer can be used for wraps such as cling film, baking paper, tin foil, and re-sealable lunch bags.
- Another drawer can contain tea towels, cleaning cloths, and perhaps table napkins.
- And of course then there's the ubiquitous bits and pieces drawer which is usually stuffed with an immense variety of objects.

One of the easiest ways to organize items in any drawer is using dividers, or insert plastic containers to hold separate objects. This particularly works with the 'junk' drawer and using containers for like items keeps drawers from becoming a mess. Such groupings can include batteries and screwdrivers, light bulbs and spare plugs, candles and matches, pens and notepads.

Pantry

Whether your pantry is large or small, it's still one of the most difficult places to keep organized. Pantries need to be cleared regularly so you can keep an eye on expiry dates. Foods with a short use by date need to be near the front so they're eaten before similar products with a longer shelf life.

The main thing with pantries is that we're accessing them every single day, and oftentimes several times a day. So it's time saving, cost saving, and saves also on frustration, if everything in your pantry is organized, easily accessible, and visible. Very often, what we see is what we use, and what we can't see we go out and buy, again!

A good rule is to store everything in obvious groups:

- Cans and non-perishables, soups and quick meals
- Herbs and spices alongside the vinegars and oils
- Cereals and spreads
- Baking ingredients: flour, baking powder, yeast, caster sugar
- Pastas, rice, legumes
- Pet food on a separate shelf [or at the bottom of the pantry]

This is such a time saver and means that whether you're baking a cake, or cooking the family meal, you know immediately where to put your hand on everything you need.

It is like filing—if foods are grouped logically, and simple to find, it'll take a lot of hassle out of cooking and preparing a meal.

Before you start organizing your pantry, first decide which shelf you are going to use for which foods. Eye-level shelves are best for most often used products. Take everything off the first shelf you're going to organize and put it all on a bench. Then start stacking like-minded items on that shelf, keeping larger things to the back and smaller to the front. Ideally you want to be able to see and to reach any item without knocking anything over, or without having to pull out things to get to those at the back, so if you have enough pantry room to allow you to place individual items alongside each other, rather than in front—that's perfect.

Stacking boxes sideways, such as cereal containers, will allow you to see what they are and make them easy to pull out.

Cluster together small items, such as herbs and spices, in a see through container—it will be easier to keep them organized together, and to see packet labels and you can also move them all to your work surface when you are about to cook saving you a number of journeys. One of Angella's clients stores her many herbs and spices in a drawer in alphabetical order—a real time saver when cooking.

Stacking systems such as wire stands or expandable shelf systems are a brilliant way to organize a pantry by keeping everything in view and easy to reach.

The larger stackable wire baskets make good use of the bottom of the pantry for veges and pet food.

Fridge / Freezer

Yes, even the fridge and freezer become cluttered and, if not cleared out regularly, can contain a few scary items such as those that have grown fur, mould, or are just plain smelly.

A simple way to organize your fridge items is to use containers which can be easily lifted out to get to what you want. Foods which can be grouped logically in containers are: cheeses, spreads, energy bars, yoghurts, and you can even separate in smaller containers your fruit and veges in the vege bin at the bottom of the fridge.

Use the same principle in the freezer, and even if you don't have a big enough freezer space to fit containers then at least organize the items so they are grouped together. Another of Angella's clients has a large freezer but it was so disorganized and full of such an assortment of foods that she couldn't find anything. Once everything had been grouped together in specific freezer compartments she could see exactly where everything was. And the bonus was that she stopped overbuying things she already had, but hadn't been able to find.

Storage

No matter how large a house, everyone complains that there isn't enough storage. Angella knew someone who was thinking of buying a bigger house because the family had so much stuff they'd almost grown out of their already large four-bedroom home. Yet, more often than not storage is there, it's just that it's poorly organized. Often spacious cupboards may contain just a few items on each shelf, which is really under-utilizing valuable storage space.

Once you have decluttered your kitchen, and pantry, you'll find storage spots appear from nowhere. This isn't new space, just space you have created by finding a more suitable home for what you already have, as well as space that was once filled with things you realized you never used and removed.

The bottom of the pantry is usually large enough to take a couple of plastic storage bins, or stackable baskets. But don't clutter this space as you still want to be able to reach everything, preferably without having to move things out of way to get to the potatoes or the kitty litter.

There is often under-used space in the pantry so it's worth taking stock of what's there, what doesn't need to be there (and could be relocated elsewhere), and how best the area can be organized.

Use high cupboards for things you don't often use such as platters and trays; party glasses; or dearly departed Gran's tea set. Make sure though that it's nothing too heavy which could make getting it down a bit perilous.

Use space between the ceiling and the top of cupboards for rarely used objects. For example, Angella has two wicker baskets with lids which sit on the top of her kitchen cupboards. One basket contains candles, candle holders and lighters; the other has her tools, nails and screws, batteries, light bulbs, picture hooks and spare plugs.

Rather than cluttering up a drawer with all of these things, which can be a nightmare to sort through, her wicker baskets are attractive and their contents are able to be neatly sorted so she can see everything at a glance.

Above all, try not to store items in the kitchen that are not necessary, or are not kitchen related as this room already has more than its fair share.

You can create storage in every room of your house with clever systems and we'll show you some ideas as we work through this book.

Remember, the best way to make your space look un-cluttered is by clearing every surface of extraneous items. Try it—take everything that doesn't need to be there off your kitchen benches. Now look at everything you've taken off these surfaces and think about what could go into a drawer, cupboard, storage box, or rubbish sack.

Case Study

Problem:

Emily called Angella in to reorganize her kitchen. She knew it wasn't working well for her, but couldn't quite figure out why. She has a beautiful large square shaped kitchen, with lots of cupboards and drawers. However, when she had moved into the house she hadn't thought about the most convenient places for everything.

All the pots and pans were on the opposite side of Emily's kitchen to her stove and bench top. One side of the double sided pantry was full of extra glasses and china that she only used on special occasions such as parties, and the other side of her pantry was cramped and poorly organized so that she couldn't find anything. This meant she kept buying food that she already had at the back of the pantry (but couldn't see): she had six or seven packets of pasta, and several bags of rice. Items such as little used serving dishes and bowls hogged a drawer which was ideal for plates.

Solution:

The lovely deep drawers under the bench top stove elements were used to store her pots and pans, along with assorted baking trays.

All extra glasses and china were stored in a box in the spare room wardrobe, leaving her with full use of her pantry for food items. The pantry was then organized so that like products were grouped together: pastas and rice on one shelf, breakfast spreads and cereals on another.

The deep drawers, where pots and pans were originally kept, are now used for all of her china, which was much more convenient because she now has clear bench space above, which is near the dining room so she can put out plates for serving and then move to the other side of the bench/servery to place them on the dining room table.

Rationale:

Emily needed a kitchen which was much more serviceable, and where everything was stored logically. We saved her a lot of time and frustration by having everything she used regularly positioned to the front of her cupboards and drawers. And we saved her money by reorganizing the pantry so she no longer over-buys products because everything in her pantry is now visible.

Overview—Angella's Laws

Safety

- Ensure there is a clear heat resistant area beside stove or elements where you can place hot pans directly from the oven.
- Oven and pot mitts should be in a handy place beside the stove and elements so you're not tempted to use a tea towel to grab a hot dish or pan from the oven.
- Microwave ovens should ideally be on a bench top, or at waist level so you're not reaching up to get hot dishes out of the microwave.
- If you have small children around keep sharp objects and knives out of view and out of reach.
- Cleaning products are often toxic—put kiddy locks on cupboard doors where these are stored, or put them in a cupboard that children can't reach.

And practicality

- Think 'uncluttered' areas, and keep working areas clear of anything that absolutely doesn't need to be there.
- Throw out or give away double ups and no longer used appliances.
- Once you're decided where everything goes, make a habit of returning items to their home after each use.
- Use containers to organize pantry and fridge items.
- Keep anything which does not relate to the kitchen out of the kitchen.
- Don't allow the kitchen bench to become a junk repository where everyone leaves keys, mail, papers, school books and miscellaneous items of clothing.
- When you've created your systems and decided on a home for everything, show the family, or flatmates, and encourage them to help you by keeping everything in its place. They'll soon see that they will benefit from your new systems as well.

A few more Tips

Keys:

Nail a quirky key holder to the wall in the room closest to the entry in the house—this may be the kitchen, hallway or entrance lobby.

Your keys need to be handy, and easy to find when leaving the house. When returning home you will soon get into the habit of using this key holder if it's put somewhere logical.

Mail:

Have a 'mail container' handy where mail and magazines can be placed until opened. A small wicker basket or tray will work and, as long as it is continually emptied, it will remain relatively uncluttered.

Kitchen stool:

These are ideal for those too high to reach cupboards. It saves dragging a chair into the kitchen every time you need something from a hard to reach cupboard or shelf, and a fold away stool cum step ladder can usually fold up and slot neatly into a corner.

Questions & Answers:

Q **Mother just died and I have inherited all of her stuff, the tea service, silver, and bone china cups and saucers. What do I do with them all when I already have my own?**

A You could make a feature of beautiful fine china and tea sets by displaying them on a shelf in the kitchen or even on a dining room wall. Or store these items in a top cupboard where you put least used items. Alternatively, if you feel you don't want to keep it all, why not donate them to a hospice or other charity shop for someone else to treasure?

Q **The door of my fridge is cluttered with kids' drawings, reminders of things to do, and shopping lists for Africa. It just looks a mess.**

A Make a lovely bright decorative display for your kitchen wall with your kids' favorite drawings by framing them in brightly colored picture frames. Get picture frames that can easily be opened up allowing pictures to be changed frequently so that each child has the pleasure of seeing their work of art well presented.

　　And for shopping lists and reminders, stick a cork board on the back of the kitchen door, or inside the pantry door. Make sure that you weed this board regularly so that it doesn't get clogged with flyers for events that have taken place, and remove out of date messages.

Q **I've recently split up from my husband of 25 years and have moved from a large family home into a smallish flat. My husband has moved in with someone else and didn't take anything from the kitchen. I have so many kitchen knick knacks that it's hard to get into a kitchen that is about the size of a broom cupboard. I now live on my own but I put my daughter up some weekends when she's home from university. Help.**

A   Sadly a fact of modern life is that I often get asked to help people in your predicament. It's easier to move up from smaller accommodation than to downsize. But it is possible. At times like these one needs to find an emotional as well as practical response. Suggesting that you have a garage sale to get rid of the kitchen equipment you used to raise a family may seem crass and insensitive if these items are full of memories for you; or you may be ready to let them go in which case a garage sale may well work for you.

Either way, we suggest you make an inventory of the kitchen equipment you will need in your present circumstances. Bear in mind also the times when you invite friends round for coffee, hold small dinner parties and so forth.

Think about what sort of cooking you plan to do for yourself. Many single people cook large meals then freeze in meal sized portions using plastic containers which you can buy in bulk from supermarkets.

Others find that it easier to buy in cakes and pastries rather than bake at home. If you realize that you are unlikely to bake you can put all your baking equipment, mixer, scales, muffin tins and the rest in a container and place out of sight, possibly in the bottom of the pantry, or the space between the top of cupboards and the ceiling, or store the container in a corner of the garage.

As discussed earlier you only want equipment you use every day near to hand which means that everything apart from a few plates, mugs, saucepans, and selection of kitchen knives need stay in your tiny kitchen while things you need when you're having a dinner party can be stored elsewhere. Large kitchens like the one you were used to often get used to store things that strictly need not be there like cleaning equipment, the iron and ironing board and even vacuum cleaner. You could for instance find homes for these things elsewhere in the flat.

An advantage of living in a flat as opposed to a house is that generally everything is on one level and you never have to walk too far to find something. Homes can be found for cleaning equipment perhaps in the bathroom or laundry, and shoe cleaning equipment can be kept in a hall cupboard or wardrobe.

Q **I live in a flat with three other flatmates, and we all buy our own food. I'm sick of going to the fridge to make a meal and finding my flatmates have already eaten what I was planning to cook. How can we organize our food so that it doesn't get mixed up with everyone else's?**

A This is where plastic containers come into their own. You can buy every size of plastic container imaginable from a supermarket, so choose four of the same size for the fridge and some more for the pantry. Label each person's containers—so each flatmate will have their own labeled containers in the fridge for their food; and they'll also have their own labeled containers in the pantry. Make sure the labels are facing outwards so you can all see which is which.

Q **My kitchen island is a huge dumping ground. The mail, newspaper, kids' school books and bags, and everything else you can think of, all get dumped on it and I have to try and clear it off before I can even start preparing a meal.**

A This is a common problem, and it's just a habit that the family's got into, so it can be changed. Everything has its place: see the tips above for what to do with the keys and mail. The kids need to be encouraged to put their school gear in their bedrooms; and ideally the junk mail and old newspapers will be dumped into the recycling bin.

   Once cleared, we suggest you create a beautiful feature on the kitchen island—it could be a vase of flowers, or a large fruit bowl. Put it in the middle of the bench so the family will see that you have created a pretty display on the island and that it's not for clutter.

Q **I have a lovely new kitchen with a gorgeous polished wood kitchen island. Unfortunately my husband insists on using the island as his work space scattering all of his papers and junk over the entire surface. When I get home from work and am faced with all of his paper and stuff on my beautiful kitchen island, it just drives me to distraction. How can I get him to tidy it up and stop using it as a dumping ground?**

A   If you don't have another space for hubby to use as his 'office', then create a system for his paperwork. You could get an archive box or container for his papers. Buy some file sleeves and bull dog clips so it's easy for him to sort everything.

He still gets to work on the bench but at the end of his work session, encourage him to gather up all of his papers and books, and put them back in the box. You might have to do it for the first couple of times, but he'll get the drift.

Conclusion

You might like to use these exercises as part of your planning process. You can use this space or you may prefer to keep your notes in an exercise book.

1. Write down five things you like about your kitchen.

_____

_____

_____

_____

_____

_____

2. Now write five things you dislike about it.

_____

_____

_____

_____

_____

_____

3.   What would you most like to change?

_____

_____

_____

_____

_____

_____

4.   Describe your ideal kitchen.

_____

_____

_____

_____

_____

_____

CHAPTER FOUR

THE HOME OFFICE

There was a time when few people worked from home and therefore didn't require a home office or study. Not anymore. The advent of domestic computers, access to the internet, emailing and other forms of contemporary communications makes a home office a must for families and individuals.

Work patterns are changing. Once almost all paid employment took place outside the home. Increasingly more and more of us are taking advantage of technology and tap away on our computers in what was once a spare bedroom, rather than jumping into a Japanese hatchback and joining the morning traffic jam. In addition the move towards lifelong learning means that latter day students can be any age from eighteen to eighty.

But of course you don't need to be a student or running a business from your residential address to benefit from having an office in your home. There are distinct advantages in centralizing domestic admin to one location and having a dedicated space for stationary. In other words having an area where everyone can share a computer and printer. In the past there was less need for a home office as writing a letter by hand could be carried out from almost anywhere. Sadly so called snail mail has largely been replaced by emails and texting, requiring a mobile telephone, PC, laptop and a connection to cyberspace. And this kit takes up space.

Most houses are not designed to include a home office. A room tends only to be given over for this purpose if there is a surplus bedroom or another room that is not fit for anything else.

While most of this book is concerned with decluttering established areas like kitchens, bedrooms or lounges, the best way to ensure that you have a properly functioning and uncluttered home office is by finding sufficient space for one. It might not be possible to have a room that is exclusively used for business, admin or home study, but there are crafty ways of separating these roles from normal domestic life ensuring there are strong boundaries.

Whether you are using this area for professional or private reasons, the decluttering principles are identical. They are no different whether you live in a mansion or a breadbox.

Using our same format as in the other chapters, we'll go through the following steps:

- Assessment
- Planning
- Implementation
- Evaluation

Assessment

Location, location, location! A spare room cum guest bedroom makes an ideal home office. Even if you still need a spare bed there is often room for a desk and other office furniture, and there's likely to be a cupboard, wardrobe and spare chest of drawers which could be roped in as office storage.

If you don't have a spare room, you will have to be inventive and find space elsewhere. An attic may be a possibility, or a partitioned portion of the garage or basement area. You can even set up your home office in a large walk in wardrobe, with a chair you can pull up to it, and which will all neatly close off when you've finished your work day.

If at all possible avoid using the bedroom you use for sleeping. Computers, modems, and printers all have glowing lights and hum which will either tempt you to keep checking your emails, or make you feel guilty that you are not working on some report or document. The bedroom is for sleeping, and other delightful activities; if your workspace is in the bedroom, then the worst parts of work will never be far from your mind. A corner of the lounge or dining room is a better bet, and with the clever use of standing screens, or tall leafy plants, you can effectively shut off the area from your living area.

Eye up the space you've chosen as your working space for your office, and decide on what it needs to contain. Do you need a filing cabinet? How big is your desk and what absolutely needs to go on it, apart from your computer? Are there cupboards you can use for storing your files and resources?

Make a list of what you think you'll need in your home office.

If your home office is already set up, but not working for you because it's horribly cluttered and definitely not efficient, stand back and assess what you see.

Ask yourself:

- Is it an efficient area that you feel is working for you?
- What are your frustrations?
- Do you have a workable filing system?
- Is there paper everywhere with no cohesive order?
- Is the home clutter encroaching on your work space, kids' toys on the desk etc?
- Is your desk so covered in paper that you don't have a clear space to work on?
- Do you have to hunt high and low for the stapler, or an elusive pen that actually works?

And most importantly:

- Do you feel good when you enter your office—does it make you feel empowered and ready to get to work?
- Or, do you look at the mountains of paper and clutter and feel anxious, full of dread or depressed?
- Is it difficult to concentrate on important tasks because of distractions?

The husband of one of Angella's clients asked his wife why Angella had to declutter his wife's home office, why couldn't she do it herself.

Apparently the wife looked at her cluttered office where every surface including the floor was covered in paper and miscellaneous objects, and just shrugged. She had decided it was far too hard for her to sort; she felt resentful and overburdened and was at the stage where she couldn't even begin to think of where to start.

But it can be done. And it doesn't have to create heartache, stress and overwhelm.

Planning

Once you've carried out a detailed assessment you have a pretty good idea of what needs to happen. Making a written list helps some people organize their thinking and there is satisfaction in scrubbing off each completed job.

If you can't complete a job in the same day give yourself a deadline for when it's going to get done.

If you're on a tight budget, it's worth finding out how much new, or second hand equipment will cost. You can rank the things you need so you buy the most important equipment first and leave optional objects until you can afford them.

The following steps apply if you haven't yet set up your home office, and also if the one you have isn't fit for this purpose.

Here's our crib sheet:

- What furniture will you need e.g. desk, office chair(s), desk lamp?
- Does the room already have shelving, or cupboards that can be used for storing files and stationery?
- Get the position of the desk right first. Move it around in different positions until you find the right spot. A good position will take advantage of natural light. If at all possible place the desk so that anyone sitting at it faces the door. This ensures that you see anyone entering the room and makes it easier to acknowledge them if you are on the telephone, and could save

you an unnecessary fright if you're concentrating and someone comes up behind you.

- If the office is doubling up and being used for another role is there any way you can screen off the area? This can be done using standing or folding screens, or even with large pot plants. In other words, you want to define the area.

Implementation

This is pretty simple. Give yourself some uninterrupted time and working off your plan start positioning furniture and the paraphernalia that needs to go into your office. Work unhurriedly, focusing on the job at hand. Keep asking the question: if I put this item here, is it going to be easy to reach and quick to access when I need it? In other words, it needs to make sense to you where you put things as this is what creates a maintainable system.

We'll deal in detail with the practical steps in setting up your office below.

Evaluation

Stand back and assess what you've done. Is the new arrangement pleasing to the eye? Is it an inviting workspace and are things you use daily near to hand? You may find that once you start using the office some aspects do not work as well as anticipated and objects and even furniture may need to be repositioned. You won't know how effective a system is until you start using it.

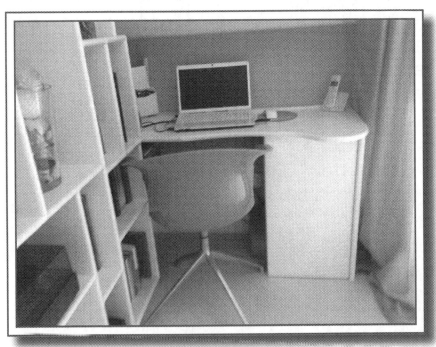

The office above is cluttered to the extent that there's no room to move, and finding something would definitely be a challenge.

Instead the office below, while tucked neatly into a corner, provides a nice uncluttered working area.

Practical Steps to Organize your Home Office

The Office Space

Setting up your home office can be a pleasurable task. Think of reasons you're doing it: time freedom, convenience of working from home, benefits of having an admin hub, and any one of a multitude of other reasons only you will know. Create a positive mindset so the process feels like fun rather than a chore.

Start with furniture placement, bearing in mind always how you are going to be working. Make sure there is easy access to your desk, that there is enough space behind it to move your chair without bumping into shelving or other furniture. Consider lighting when positioning a desk. Near a window could be an advantage however some people prefer not to have a view out the window as they find it distracting and it can lead to daydreaming.

Once the desk is in position you can start moving outwards, or sideways if you like. *Angella has her office desk against one wall, with tall shelving/cupboard units on each side for easy storage of files and resource material. Her printer and computer tower sit neatly underneath her desk on a small shelving unit.*

Tip: **If you don't already have a desk, think about getting one which will allow things to be stored underneath it, such as printer, computer tower, maybe a small 2-drawer filing cabinet. You want to maximize your space as much as possible.**

A smart solution where space is limited is to use a standalone 'deep' cupboard, perhaps with a shelf at the ideal height for your computer and keyboard, with the bottom half of the cupboard used for storage. You can simply draw your chair up to the open doors when you're working, and when you've finished you can close the doors and forget about work. You could also create something along these lines by converting a walk in wardrobe, as mentioned earlier in this chapter.

Why is it that a home office is so often the drabbest room in the house: a mishmash of clashing colors and no decorating scheme? Just because you work here and it's a part of the home that visitors don't see doesn't mean it should look as attractive as a charity shop. Perhaps it dates back to the story of Adam and Eve when hard work became a punishment for disobedience. Make your home office an attractive and welcoming room to work in and your productivity will improve dramatically.

Second hand filing cabinets can be transformed by spraying with a color that complements the overall color scheme. Rugs, pictures and good lighting can all play their part in making your home office somewhere you enjoy being. After all you need something pleasing to look at when you need a rest from the computer screen.

However you decide to decorate and organize your office, the caveat here is to keep as much as possible off your desk so don't clutter it with photo frames and the kids' latest school projects, no matter how cute they are.

The Desk

We've spoken about the desk, and this is where we want to hammer home that your desk is your working area. This means you want it to be as clear and uncluttered as possible. A cluttered desk is a distraction, and makes it harder to focus on the task in hand.

In an ideal world the desk should contain your computer, a container for pens, a note pad, the file or files that you're currently working on, and your phone. This may sound impractical and even impossible but if you try it, you'll find the word efficiency takes on a new meaning

Mastering the Paper

Decide once and for all that you're going to get rid of all those little scrappy pieces of paper that are littering your desk. You can use a bulletin board, or whiteboard, to capture any reminder notes. Bulletin boards are useful, however they can also become very messy if not culled regularly. A whiteboard can often look cleaner and you can use little magnetic buttons to attach notes to the board, as well as using your whiteboard pens to scribble reminders.

Another way to use your bulletin board is to pin up your To Do list for the day. Angella prints out her weekly schedule from Microsoft Outlook (the Calendar option) as she likes to see her week at a glance, and at the same time she can easily add meetings and to do items to the schedule.

An alternative method for handling those bits of paper: an A4 size spiral bound notebook works well for jotting down ideas, and making notes (rather than using post-it notes or slips of paper). Your notebooks can be stored in a cupboard or desk drawer so you don't lose the information. Names and numbers that you've jotted down on a scrap of paper can be entered into your database, into your Smartphone, or write them down in your spiral notebook.

The idea here is to get rid of all the pieces of paper on your desk, and we strongly suggest you don't bunch them all up and throw them into a drawer either.

Desk Drawers

These become as nightmarish as the surface of the desk. It doesn't matter how many drawers you have, they need to be organized so each drawer has its own designated function.

The top drawer is the most useful for small often used stationery items—in other words this is where you put those bits and pieces you had on top of your desk such as the papers clips, stapler etc. Other drawers may contain current client files, writing pads and copy paper, and business cards. Or you may have a dedicated drawer for drop files.

Desk drawer organizers, or trays, neatly handle all those small miscellaneous items, and they slot neatly into the drawer. If you don't have an organizer you can line up two or three shallow plastic containers in the drawer which will do the trick of containing and categorizing these items.

Another idea for those loose bits and pieces is medium size square baskets which can sit neatly side by side onto a nearby shelf to keep miscellaneous small items contained in one place.

Business Cards

It's worth briefly focusing here on business cards—every man and his dog seems to have a business card these days, and before you know it a whole drawer has been filled with them. It saves so much valuable time if you have a filing system for business cards so that you're not ratting around in a drawer for your plumber's card while water is rapidly flooding the kitchen floor.

Or better still, employ a student [or your teenager] and ask them to type the contact information on each card into your database. You can then scrap the cards completely.

Computer Cables

Wouldn't we love to be able to do away with all the spaghetti of cords which hangs around on the floor under the desk, and ultimately under our feet.

More often now technology is becoming cordless, however there are still those of us who have a veritable forest of cords behind our computer to deal with.

Here are some ideas on how to contain your computer cables so they are not a peril:

- Cable clips or cable ties that wrap around a group of cables. The cable clips can usually be opened up and then closed again so you can modify your set up over time. Most cable ties lock together for security and are designed for one time use, so would need to be replaced if opened.

- Reusable Velcro straps are similar to cable clips and may be easier for some people to open and close.

Filing Solutions: Cabinet, Drawers or a Cupboard

There are various filing solutions now which work superbly and can negate the need for the sort of heavy metal filing cabinet that could dominate a room and look out of place in a domestic setting. If like Angella you are working within a small area which doubles up as a living area, and don't want an unsightly filing cabinet in the room, consider some alternative space-saving solutions.

If you'd rather have your office files and miscellaneous bits and pieces neatly out of sight, a nifty little two or three door cupboard could sit happily alongside a desk and they are both attractive and functional.

All those little office stationery bits and pieces like scotch tape, labels, highlighters and staples (which are usually floating around our desks) can go into a container, which can then slip neatly into the cupboard or drawers.

The beauty of using a cupboard or shelving unit for your filing solutions is that they can be relatively small pieces of furniture but with decent capacity, and would not look out of place if your office is in a semi public area.

The sort of filing system you adopt will depend on what you need the office for. If you have a busy consulting practice with a large number of client files and a plethora of resource material, you may need a two or three-drawer filing cabinet. If so, have your filing cabinet close enough to the desk to provide access. Make sure there is sufficient space to open a drawer fully without banging into anything or grazing your shins, and ensure it is conveniently facing towards you to avoid the need to do acrobats to retrieve a file.

Most families and individuals are unlikely though to have such extensive filing requirements and more and more people are moving towards the ideal of a semi-paperless office and tend to store their information electronically.

More Filing Solutions

Vertical magazine files are fantastic for stacking files. Not being a fan of filing cabinets, Angella uses these for many of her filing needs. These are much more convenient for filing than the horizontal filing trays we usually see on desks which fast become the dreaded overflowing in-tray, as the vertical file container can sit neatly on the side of your desk without taking up a lot of room, and they're tidy. Angella also has a few of these magazine files stored in a cupboard by her desk, for resource material, periodicals, and files she doesn't need to access as often.

A4 L-shaped Pocket files are firm enough to stand up in a vertical magazine file. They open at the top and right side-edge for easy access, and being transparent plastic you can immediately see the contents. As they come in a variety of colors you can create categories for different files and label each file (a sticky label in the corner or even a post-it note inside the front of the file will suffice). This system takes care of everything that is normally found in an in-tray. The paper instantly becomes contained and more manageable and by color coding your files you can easily find them without having to rummage through awkward horizontal in-trays.

Suspension files which slot into a specific file container are also a good option, and these containers can take as many as 10 drop files. They work just as well as a filing cabinet, and as they're not unwieldy the whole file container can easily slot into a cupboard or onto a shelf.

Concertina files are really useful for filing important household documents such as legal papers, mortgage documents, insurance, medical papers, and vehicle documents. They have different types of indexes so you can get one to suit your type of filing system. And of course they will fit neatly into a cupboard or onto a shelf near the desk.

Shelving

Shelving makes it so easy to organize everything, and keep your desk clear, while ensuring you can locate documents quickly. The trick here is to set up a cohesive system so that everything is immediately visible while still maintaining a tidy, uncluttered look.

A word of warning though, if you're going to stack paper and files on the shelves that you simply want to get off your desk, without using any system, then your office is still going to look a mess. However, if the papers and files are neatly stacked into containers or file boxes then you've created a system which looks neat and tidy, and as long as the file boxes are labeled then you will also know exactly where to put your hand on any file or piece of paper.

Tailor your shelving. Shelves that are so high that you need a step ladder, or high heels, should only be used for documents you rarely require otherwise you will be wasting lots of time and energy that could be better spent. Likewise shelves near the floor should only be used for storing infrequently needed or archived documents.

Archiving

Do take some time to go through material and files you keep in your office to sort what can be archived. While it's a fact that we have to keep certain papers for a number of years, we certainly don't need to have old files cluttering up our workspace.

Once you're decided what can be archived, and this will include past financial year accounts and the like, sort them into labeled storage boxes. You can even opt for different colored archive boxes so you can color code your files making retrieval really fast.

Whether you get the large square archive boxes, or the flatter version, they can all stack on top of each other and be stored in an attic, garage cupboard or shelf, or even in the spare wardrobe. Make sure the labeled side of each box is facing outwards when you store them away.

Tip: **Before archiving old client files, jot down the client contact details and a description of the job and add them to your database. This way you're not rifling around in archive boxes looking for that past client file just so you can retrieve the details of the person you dealt with on the project and their phone number.**

Resource Material

The most important thing here is to be able to access your resource material quickly and efficiently—if you have to hunt high and low for an article, or information on a CD or external hard drive, chances are you'll give up and move on to something else, or spend ages searching the Internet for information that you know you've already printed out and 'filed somewhere'. Searching for anything, especially when you're in a hurry, gets to be an exercise in frustration.

Storage boxes can work well for resource material, or you could use the plastic files and vertical file containers if you're storing articles, clippings, or magazines. And a handsome shelving system for resource books is functional as well as decorative.

Other storage ideas

Stationery is often something that gets dumped all over the office, and reams of copy paper are often found underneath other stacks of paper and files. It's not uncommon for Angella to find several opened reams of copy paper in a client's office—*"I couldn't find any paper for the printer so I went out and bought some more"*.

Have a central area for all of your stationery items, from spare paper and files, right down to paper clips and staples. Delegate a shelf, drawer or even an archive box, for spare paper and files, indexes and plastic pockets. Smaller stationery items such as spare pens, staples, paper clips, glue and scotch tape, can fit neatly into a separate box, and you can fit smaller boxes into this box to contain the tiny items (i.e. drawing pins and paper clips) so you're not scrabbling around searching for a paper clip in the bottom of a box or drawer.

Ladder storage is funky and functional, and can be tucked into a corner for stacks of books or file boxes.

A two or three drawer unit is attractive and useful for stationery items, copy paper, plastic sleeves, note pads etc.

A slim line set of shelves could take resource magazines, or a decorative storage box for stationery.

A home office doesn't have to look bland to be functional. By using attractive storage systems, hanging a favorite picture on the wall, and keeping the clutter at bay, you'll create a pleasant and welcoming environment and actually enjoy your office, rather than dreading the chore of tackling the endless paper nightmare to get to your desk.

Case Study

Scott Johnson works from home and has been doing so for the past three years. He converted his conservatory into an office when he decided to move away from corporate life and set up his own company selling office furniture to large and small firms. He spends part of his week travelling round the country visiting prospective and existing customers but most of the time works from home on his own.

"I thought very hard about how I wanted to work from home and took out a few friends who already did so and plied them with beer getting them to tell me about the pros and cons. Some of these guys seemed to love it while others felt they had little choice. I got the impression that you could easily fall into the trap of working all the time and getting burnt out or finding things to do around the house and never doing anything.

Anyway I discussed it with my wife, as I do with everything else, and she was supportive even though she wasn't sure whether some of my suggestions made sense. So when I walk into my office I'm at work. Some people might think I've lost the plot, but I dress up to go to work which in my case means putting on a crisp clean shirt and a suit. Of course I could work in my pajamas and nobody at the other end of a phone would know, but I would and I wouldn't feel in the right frame of mind. Occasionally I have to pop out to meet a client or sometimes someone comes to meet me here so it helps to be dressed appropriately but that's not the main reason: I dress to feel in work mode.

As time has gone on I have relaxed a bit and have the odd day when I dress in more casual wear but even city offices have dress down days. I keep regular hours. I aim to be sitting behind my desk by eight thirty and see if I can work through the email backlog by nine when the phone starts ringing. When I started working from home I installed a business telephone line and this is the only number I give to clients. It might be different for others but I need a buffer between my home and work life, switching back and forth does my head in.

When I started I had to be really firm with the kids and tell them that when the office door was closed I was at work and they couldn't disturb me. They tried to at first and got a bit upset when I told them I would see them later but they soon got the message. This might seem a bit harsh but in a sense I'm no different from any other dad who works in a down town office. In the past three years there has only been one emergency when Charlie came off his bike and I had to take him to the local casualty and I was really glad I was on the spot.

As far as possible once I get to work I try to stay here and avoid returning to the rest of the house. I've got a coffee machine here and as I drink it black I don't have an excuse to go to the kitchen for milk. It also works the other way. On days when I am not out visiting customers, I clock off at five and put on the answer phone and change into something casual. Sometimes there has been a report that couldn't wait till the next day to finish so I put in a few extra hours but generally I try not to let my work intrude into my family life.

I am also a school governor and have been roped in to produce the PTA newsletter so I do that task here at home but I make sure that I do it outside my office hours otherwise things would get confused. Would I ever go back to working in a team sales office like I was before? That's a difficult question. You can never say never, but for the time being the present arrangements suits me just fine."

Overview—Angella's Laws

Health & Safety

- False economies versus comfort: get a really good office chair, don't use the spare kitchen chair. Your back will thank you for this.
- Loads of messy paper, particularly when on the floor, will sometimes attract crawling insects *(Angella's come across the odd cockroach or two, dead and alive, in a client's cluttered office).* Keep paper whether it's files, resource material or copy paper, in a container, drawer or cabinet.
- You can't clean your office if it's so cluttered that you can't vacuum or dust properly.
- Make sure the area or room is not damp—get a dehumidifier or open the windows as often as possible.
- Tie up computer cables and plugs so you are not falling over them.

And practicality

- Uncluttered surfaces in a home office will allow you to work with a clear mind.
- Filing systems for everything in your home office are vital, take the time to set up well labeled systems.
- Efficient organized systems will also save you time and money—as you're creating your systems remember to place those items you use most often closest to your desk.
- Create well defined areas in your office, especially if the area is used by others in the family (see the Q&A below on this point).
- Desk drawers have a habit of becoming very cluttered, especially the drawer where you keep those small miscellaneous stationery items—pop organizers or small containers into the desk drawer to keep these items together.
- Do archive material (if it needs to be kept) and store labeled archive boxes in a cupboard.

Questions & Answers

Q **I live in a large bedsit, isn't it fanciful to talk about a home office?**

A Why not get one of those fold away cabinets that when opened out becomes a computer desk and also houses admin, files, stationery etc (as mentioned earlier in this chapter).

Q **I have a small office, a box room at the top of the house. It feels claustrophobic and bursting at the seams with bookcases full of old files and junk connected to client jobs that have accumulated since I set up my contracting business nine years ago. I wish there was a larger room in the house I could move into but there isn't. Help.**

A Have you thought of archiving those old records—stack them all into a plastic storage bin and store it in the garage. Then go through everything else to define what you really need in your office now, and remove the rest. Once you've cleared everything out you should be left with a fairly clear space. You can then look at how you can create an efficient and comfortable office area, perhaps paint the walls to brighten it up, and put some prints on the wall.

Set your working area and desk up so that you're making best use of the space. You can use the bookcases for your filing systems, but don't just dump the files onto the shelves—get some colored file boxes which will also allow you to categorize all your paperwork i.e. file by client/job, admin papers, resources, stationery, financials and marketing materials.

Q **I'd love to have a home office but with six kids, two dogs, and three cats, there is no way I could find enough space. I was recently made redundant and I'm starting my own coaching business. What do you suggest?**

A   With such a large family of people and animals I take it you also
have a fairly large stand alone house. Is there any way you could get
a conservatory built onto the side of the house, or perhaps you have
a garden shed which could be done up.

The advantage of having a completely separate area from the
main house is that you have a readymade buffer between home
and work. If you decided to use the garden shed, you could get the
electricity put on so you can also make yourself a coffee, and heat
the place in the winter.

Q   **Our home office has to accommodate not only my work,
but also my husband's, so our files get mixed up and I have
to clear the desk after he's used it so I can get some work
done. I also have two businesses and don't know how to keep
files, resources, and accounts and receipts for each of them
separate.**

A   This is a classic situation where everything needs to be clearly
categorized. In the case of your work and your husband's—create
an area in the office where each of you has a set of drawers or a
cupboard each for your files. At the end of each work session, make
a pact to clear the desk for the next person, even if you pick up
all of your papers and pop them into a drawer in your designated
cabinet.

The same rule applies to your two businesses—you need to treat
them as separate entities and therefore store files and material for
each in different areas. Again, a separate cupboard or file drawers
should be designated for each business, and labeled as such. If you
use in-trays, then label each tray as to which business it relates to.

Conclusion

Please address the following questions as fully and as honestly as you can. Use an exercise book if you prefer.

1. If you have a home office what do you like and dislike about it? How do you think it could be improved?

_____

_____

_____

_____

_____

_____

2. What are the things that bother you the most, and that you know are affecting your efficiency?

_____

_____

_____

_____

_____

_____

3. If you haven't got a home office and feel you'd love a working area in your home, what are the essential prerequisites you think you would need, and how do you think you could accommodate these?

_____

_____

_____

_____

_____

_____

CHAPTER FIVE

BEDROOMS

The bedroom is often our sanctuary away from the madness of a family and the rest of the household responsibilities. It's where we rest and re-energize, contentedly snuggle under the covers on a cold rainy Winter's night, and where we make love.

For some of us a bedroom is our favorite place in the house, a place to curl up with a good novel, and for others their bedroom may also be where they meditate. In other words, it's our very personal space.

We're going to look at different types of bedrooms in average sized homes: from master bedroom, to those for teenagers and toddlers, and the guest room. Each of these rooms will have different needs, depending on its occupant. For example, Mum and Dad may have added a lovely squishy armchair in their bedroom where they retreat with a sigh of relief and relax with that great novel.

Teens may have a desk for their computer, sound system, and assorted 'teenage stuff', while younger kids will have some type of shelving, or bookcases, for their various projects and school work. Toddlers and babies need a space for disposable nappies, and toys and books.

And last but not least the guest room is hopefully a nice welcoming area for family and friends to stay a night or two, with a bit of wardrobe and shelving space for their gear. Each of these types of bedrooms therefore needs its own systems and organization.

Potential clutter problem areas within each bedroom can be many, again depending on the occupant, however generally these will include: wardrobe, drawers/tall boy, shelves, bedside tables and storage ability or lack of it.

Applying our usual formula, we're going to address each type of bedroom under the headings:

- Assessment
- Planning
- Implementation
- Evaluation

Assessment

Get your pad and paper ready for the assessment process, and make notes on each of the bedrooms in your house before you go onto the planning process. Create a separate notes page for each room so you'll be able to tackle one room at a time when it comes to the planning process.

Teenagers' and school age children's bedrooms are usually the scariest—they have not yet mastered any kind of organizational abilities and (in Angella's experience) everything usually gets thrown on the floor. So, gird your loins, and know that at the end of this process you will have nailed some good hardy systems and methods for keeping some form of order in your darling ones' rooms.

Master Bedroom

Stand back in the doorway of your bedroom and get a good overall picture of it. Notice if there is clutter over every surface and the floor, or do you just have a few little problem areas.

Here's what to make a note of:

- In an ideal world how would you love your room to look?
- Is furniture in the best position? Is one side of the bed up against a wall so one of you has to climb over the other to get in or out of bed? (*Yes, we've seen bedrooms like that*).
- Do you have enough drawer space for both of you? Do you each have a chest of drawers or are you struggling to share a single set?
- Are clothes draped over a bedroom chair, or stacked on the floor?
- Is your wardrobe so full of his and her clothes that it takes you 20 minutes each morning to figure out what you can wear to work?
- Are your bedside tables so covered in junk you barely have space for your current book or reading glasses?
- Do you have good lighting and preferably lamps on each side of the bed?
- Hopefully you haven't got your computer in your bedroom, and if you have, read the chapter on "Home Office" ideas to see where else it can go.

Teenager's room

Fingers crossed this hasn't been declared a "no parent zone" by your teenager . . . we find if you consult your teen on the process and ask for their input you'll probably get the cooperation you need. Ideally, ask your teenager to do their room with you—explain what you're doing with the rest of the house (so they don't think you're zeroing in on them and their sloppy habits); and that you're making a plan to ensure their bedroom answers their needs, as well as yours.

What do you both see as actual problem areas:

- Is the furniture placement ideal for the space?
- Is there too much furniture in the room, or too little?
- Would they put things away if they had adequate space and storage?
- Is there something missing they would find useful like shelving, an extra cupboard, or storage containers?
- Is there a dedicated space for their computer, sound system and CDs/DVDs?

Remember, it is your teenager who lives in the room so they're will be aware of any frustrations and current limitations and may have some good suggestions to improve it.

School Age children's rooms

Most school age children have lots of belongings and treasures which will generally be scattered over every surface, along with toys and books that they've had forever.

Like young adults, children of school age will also have formed opinions about how they'd like their room to be, and to look, so listen to them to establish what they want rather than imposing what you think is best. Chat with them about what you'd like to do and see what suggestions they have. This will engender ownership from your child while also instilling a sense of pride in their room, and reinforce good habits for the ongoing maintenance of their room.

Here's what to look for:

- Are there books and toys which have long since been discarded, or are now too young for your child, and which you could give to other willing hands?
- Is there 'baby' furniture in the room that your school age child has outgrown?

- Does existing furniture and shelving/cupboards serve your child's current needs?
- Is there a space and a suitable desk and chair where he/she can do homework?
- Where does their school bag go? Can room be made in the wardrobe for school bags?
- Is there a system for clothes and shoes? Space in the wardrobe/drawers for folded clothes?
- What happens when your kids want to bring their friends home to play—do they tend to trash the room; is there space in the room for them to play?

Toddlers/Babies

Toddlers and babies have different needs and slightly different types of storage areas.

- Is the bed or cot easy to access or do you skirt around other furniture to get to it?
- Is there adequate drawer space for toddlers' clothes; do drawers perhaps contain clothes which your toddler has long grown out of?
- Is there shelving or cupboard space for nappies, bibs, wipes etc which is orderly and quick and easy for you to grab in a hurry?
- Are there containers for toys that the child can see as a 'home' for his playthings?
- Have you culled toys and books that the child no longer uses or loves?
- What is there on the floor which could be placed on a shelf, in a cupboard, or hung on the back of a door?
- Where is the heater? Is it in a safe place where it can't be knocked over?
- Is this a room your child enjoys playing in, or do all his toys end up in other parts of your house, such as lounge, dining room and/or the kitchen?

Guest Room

So often this room becomes a junk room. Angella has seen a spare room or two where it was impossible to get in the door because the room was choc a block with stuff, from spare furniture to clothes, and even tools. You may not have people come to stay very often, however it is nice if the room is ready for unexpected guests who may decide to stay the night after a particularly long and enjoyable dinner party where everyone has imbibed a little too much.

Therefore, you want to take a good look at this room and see its possibilities:

- Would you feel comfortable offering the room to a friend or family member staying overnight (or longer), or would you be too embarrassed to even own up that you've got a spare room?
- Have you got too much furniture, some of which you're storing in this room, that could perhaps be listed on Trade Me or EBay?
- Is the room full of 'stuff' because you've been using it as a store room?
- Could the room have other uses such as a home office, homework area for the kids, craft room, or library?
- Is there space for a guest's luggage, and space to hang up one or two items of clothing?

Planning

It's vital to take one room at a time otherwise you could become overwhelmed.

Choose a room to work on, and start planning:

- Is there anything you need to buy: a piece of furniture or bedside lamp?
- Do you need to put up shelving?

- What storage have you got: under the bed, on top of the wardrobe?
- Do you need to buy storage containers?

Decide when you're going to get started on the first room, and make sure you've got plenty of uninterrupted time. Bedrooms can take time to sort and organize and it's always preferable to have a clear run at the task so you can give it all your focus.

Implementation

You may need to start by pulling things out of the bedroom to get a clear run at it so you might want to use a couple of big boxes—for example, one for clothes that are piled on the floor and bed, and another for toys. Angella tells of instances where she's had to throw everything from the floor onto the kids' bunks so she had a working space to move the other furniture around, and start creating systems.

Follow the steps below and if it feels like a chore remind yourself that time spent sorting out this room now will save you or someone else hours of effort and frustration down the line. Keep a clear picture in your mind of what the room is going to look like, and especially think about the enjoyment and sense of achievement you're going to feel when you're finished.

Evaluation

This may or may not have been a cooperative process with other members of the family. Whether you did it all yourself, or whether you had willing hands to help move furniture and sort through the stuff, now's the time to check in with family—partner and children—and get their feedback.

- Ask them how they feel about their newly decluttered room.
- Is it easier to find things, and put them away again?

- Have you noticed that they're putting things away, leaving their school bag in a designated corner of their wardrobe, tucking their shoes away neatly?
- Has your partner stopped throwing clothes over your favorite armchair in the bedroom?

It may take a little time, and a little reminding, however it's well worth educating your family into new habits in maintaining what is essentially their own domain within the house.

Tap into their self interest and help them see that what you've done in decluttering their bedroom is make more room to study, play, relax, and to create systems whereby they're going to be able to find that missing sock or shoe in an instant, as well as having a more inviting place to take friends.

Practical Steps to Declutter and Organize Bedrooms

Master Bedroom

Now you have your plan you're ready to make a start. Make sure everything is off the floor before you start—pile things on top of the bed if necessary to give you floor space to work on.

Enlist some help if you have to move heavy furniture, such as the bed or chest of drawers. If moving the bed think about access to both sides of the bed, as well as lighting. You will want to have power points near the bed for bedside lamps.

Lighting

Lighting in your bedroom serves a number of purposes: reading in bed, applying makeup or checking yourself out in a mirror, ambient lighting for a romantic mood, and good lighting when you're cleaning.

It's useful to be able to turn out the main light from your bed, or turn on bedside lamps when you get into bed so you don't have to get up to turn off a main light.

Drawers

Now the ideal is for each person to have their own set of drawers for clothes, although not all bedrooms have sufficient space to allow for this. If this is the case, you may have to utilize wardrobe space for some garments such as heavy sweaters which take up a lot of room in drawers.

Oftentimes a male will not use as many drawers as a female, mainly because they hang most of their clothing such as trousers, jeans, and shirts. Items they would put into drawers are generally t-shirts and sweatshirts, underwear, pajamas and socks. In a decent sized chest of drawers this can potentially be handled in two drawers.

Women definitely need more room as they tend to have more clothes anyway. They may also wish to use drawers for accessories such as scarves and belts, and of course they'll need a couple of drawers for lingerie, sportswear and sleepwear. And in actual fact, sometimes one set of drawers isn't even enough! However, many items can be hung or stored in the wardrobe. We'll come to that in a moment.

The main thing is that you keep each drawer specific to the person, and specific to the type of items. In other words, don't throw underwear and socks in with t-shirts or it will quickly become a messy jumble and you'll be hunting for matching socks amongst a lot of other unrelated articles.

Wardrobe

If you're lucky enough to have a designer modular wardrobe, then you are blessed. If you have a wardrobe system which has hanging areas alongside shelving (and hopefully there will be 'his and hers' shelving on each side of the wardrobe), then it's simple to organize. Of course there are many of us who don't have fancy wardrobe systems but you can still apply the rules below.

Segregate your wardrobe so you each have your own area of hanging space and shelving. Hang garments together by type: suits, jackets, trousers, skirts, shirts, sweaters and cardigans. This makes it very simple in the morning when selecting what to wear.

In the case of a simple old fashioned wardrobe which only has a rail for hanging clothes, then you can use one of various basket-type solutions which sit on the wardrobe floor and can contain neatly stacked and folded sweaters, sports clothes, and accessories.

Tips

- Face hangers and garments in the same direction so when you are sifting through it makes the selection process even quicker.
- Don't hang clothes on top of each other as you won't wear what you can't see.
- Make sure your wardrobe doesn't contain out of season clothes which you can store elsewhere, or clothes that are too small or too large. You need to be able to move coat hangers from side to side so you can get a good look at what's there, and to allow air to circulate among your clothes.

Modular wardrobes often have a space for shoes, which may be shelves or cubby holes. However if your wardrobe doesn't have dedicated 'shoe areas', there are many different types of shoe organizers to choose from. These systems look after your shoes and keep them orderly (and it's much better than having them lying on top of each other in the bottom of the wardrobe or getting dusty under your bed).

Some of the clever ideas for storing shoes include: shoe box size transparent plastic containers which you can stack on shelves; standing racks which can sit on the floor of a wardrobe; and a system of hanging shoe pockets which could either hang in the wardrobe, or behind a door.

Bedside Tables

Take everything off bedside tables, then put back only what you need when you're in bed: bedside lamp (if it isn't a wall one), a current book you're reading, reading glasses, clock, and glass of water. That's probably all you need on a bedside table. These are classic clutter areas and you really don't want a pile of clutter level with your head on the pillow when you're looking for a restful night's sleep.

Shelving

Again, try to refrain from cluttering any shelves you have in a bedroom. Bedroom shelves are useful for your favorite books, maybe pretty containers for jewellery, and something decorative such as a vase of beautiful silk flowers.

Storage

Storage can frequently be found at the top of wardrobes, occasionally under the bed, and even artfully placed in a corner. So what can you put in a storage container: anything and everything that you don't use on a regular basis such as out of season clothes and shoes, sports gear and spare linen.

We now have a huge variety of containers to choose from. These include large plastic boxes with a clip on lid which you can stack in a spare room wardrobe or the garage. These containers can take larger items, as well as archived files and papers.

Then there are the many decorative and quite lovely storage boxes which can store accessories (scarves, belts, jewellery, etc). These boxes can stack nicely on the floor in a corner, or on a shelf. The main thing about decorative storage boxes is that you don't have to hide them away. They work beautifully as a display feature in any room.

These storage solutions will work in other bedrooms as well. Think about what can be stored away and what is the most practical storage method.

Vacuum seal space bags are also a terrific idea for storing linen, blankets, and even pillows and cushions. They compress quite flat which increases your storage ability, whether under the bed or on top of a wardrobe.

Teenager's Room

If you're very lucky your teen will be helping you declutter his/her room with you. If so, allocate tasks from your plan so that you're working together but each on different parts of the room. Clear everything off the floor and move any items of furniture that you've decided would be better placed in another area. This may be to access better lighting, or to create more ease of movement in the room.

Lighting and Power Points

Ensure you take into consideration lighting and power outlets, and that there are no cords running across the floor. If there is a computer and a sound system in this room then make sure leads are tied up so they are not an untidy mass of spaghetti. (The Chapter on Home Offices has ideas on how to handle computer cords and leads).

Drawers and Wardrobe

Teens are not known to be particularly concerned about maintenance of their clothes, and in most houses we've been into with teens, their clothes are generally dumped on the floor (dirty and clean clothes). A laundry hamper is definitely useful to sort dirty clothes from those that are clean.

Allocate items so that they make a logical sense in drawers, i.e. underwear, socks and sleep wear in top drawers, with lower drawers containing t-shirts, sweatshirts and jeans.

Some teens don't bother hanging their clothes in the wardrobe, probably for no other reason than laziness. If the wardrobe is organized to make sense to him/her they might deign to use it. Categorize their clothes as described for the Master Bedroom so that it becomes clear that they can grab an item of clothing on the run.

The wardrobe floor can be used for shoe organizers and perhaps a couple of plastic bins. Bins are useful for larger items which there may not be room to hang, such as windbreakers, or sports gear.

Desk

Many teens have a desk in their bedroom for homework, computer, and often their stereo, as well as everything else that goes with those items. And their desks often look like a hurricane has swept through and upended everything. This is where containers come in handy.

Use boxes which will stack on top of each other as space savers, to gather together such items as:

- CDs and DVDs
- Computer software and Games
- Assorted gear such as ear phones, and any other electrical gear

Magazine stands, cubes, or stackable boxes can stand beside or under the desk for their magazines, books, and even papers which can be gathered into plastic sleeves as mentioned in the Home Office chapter, and popped into a box or cube.

Shelving and Storage

All sorts of systems for storage are now available, and apart from various types of boxes described above, cube units are attractive and don't take up a lot of room. They are a great solution for containing a lot of miscellaneous gear which may otherwise lie around the floor.

Remember, as with other rooms, that no longer used or wanted items are either given or thrown away, and less often used items are stored in bins or containers which may fit in the bottom or on top of the wardrobe, or under the bed.

School Age children's room

You will have by now assessed whether your child's room still contains the baby table and chairs that he had when he was a tot—and can't actually fit into now he's a big boy.

This room will follow the same principles as previous rooms, and again, we suggest you go through the process of decluttering this room with your child. As mentioned above, if you ask for your child's opinion and ask them to help you, they'll feel very grown up and proud and you can have fun working in their room together.

At the end of this chapter, under More Tips there is a section on giving away outgrown toys and books. Ask your children how they feel about this. Encourage them to give away, or sell, what they know they don't use or love anymore.

Hoarding can begin at an early age so if we are able to discourage our children from picking up this habit we will be doing them a huge favor in the future. Another of Angella's clients had a chat with her young boys about having to get rid of the old to let the new in. She also got them to picture their bedrooms in five years time if they didn't give anything away. And they got it.

Beds and Bunks

If there's more than one child sharing the room, bunks are ideal and kids love them. However, they can also be dumping grounds for all manner of objects when kids get home from school, or when they have their friends over to play.

Once you've decluttered their room, suggest your child choose one or two of their favorite stuffed animals to display in the centre of the bed, and let them know that this is the animals' space when they're not sleeping so it needs to be nice and tidy.

Drawers and Wardrobe

Sort the drawers and wardrobe much as for the teenager's room, teaching your child how to sort his clothes in each drawer, and how to hang things in the wardrobe.

Keep a corner of the wardrobe for school bags—these could go in a cube container on the floor of the wardrobe.

Desk and Shelves

If your child does his homework in the room then a desk should snugly fit against a wall in a corner, to take up as little room as possible. Do get containers for your child to keep their pencils, pens and crayons, and organize his desk so that there's as little clutter as possible. Remember, toys are going into containers on the floor and books on shelves or in a container so there shouldn't be too many items on the desk. He needs room to spread out and do his homework.

Shelves are perfect for books and a few favorite toys. If there are no shelves perhaps you could invest in cube shelving. They are fabulous for books, games and any breakable toys that won't go into containers.

Storage

This is often a big issue in a school child's room. They have school bags, homework and projects, toys, books and often huge quantities of Lego. A home needs to be found for each category. Plastic storage bins that can sit alongside each other along one wall are useful—leave lids off the bins so your child can easily access items and also instantly see where to put them back. Containers are great for storage of:

- Toys—hard and soft toys
- Lego and its related instruction booklets
- Books (if there are no book shelves in the room)

One of Angella's client's followed her advice on getting containers for her boys' toys and said: "I gathered up some of the toys in the lounge and started filling some containers up with groups of 'like' toys and it's been marvelous. The boys are completely into putting things away in them and knowing where each toy and game is supposed to go."

Toddlers and Infants Room

A toddler will have different furniture needs, such as a cot, changing table, and a good wardrobe and shelving unit for many items which need to be handy in this bedroom.

You want to keep toys off the floor of a toddler's room so that your little one doesn't fall and hurt himself, and so that Mum doesn't slip or slide on an object when checking on baby in the middle of the night. Using storage containers, like wicker baskets, will also work for toddlers.

You can create games with your little one to teach them to pick up their toys and put them away, or sing a song as you do it together.

While doing your assessment of this room you will have noted any changes you wanted to make with furniture in the room, and what else may be needed.

Drawers, cupboards and shelves need to be organized in such a way that you can reach for something in a hurry, whether it be talc or baby wipes, or disposables. A small plastic lined rubbish bin is useful beside the change table for dirty disposables as you change baby.

The Guest Room

A spare room aka guest room will often be used for storage. There's no reason why you can't do this, however ideally items you store in this room will be contained and organized so they're not encroaching on the space. It can be unpleasant to sleep in someone's spare room which is so cluttered that there's hardly room to make your way to the bed, let alone have any hope of a peaceful night's sleep with all that clutter around.

It is nice to have some empty drawers and wardrobe space in a guest room so those staying a bit longer than a night or two can hang and put their clothes away.

A bedside lamp is also good—Angella says this is something she misses (as an avid reader in bed) when she stays at her sister's house as the guest room has no lamp so the room is fully lit as she's reading (rather than having the more gentle muted light of a lamp) and she has to get out of bed to turn the light out.

If you are using the wardrobe for storing some of your containers of out of season clothes etc, stack containers to one side of the wardrobe, leaving a portion of hanging space for the guest's clothes.

Leave some space in the wardrobe also for your visitor's overnight bag, or if it's a suitcase then maybe this will slide under the bed.

You may have designated this room as your home office, kids' homework room, or craft room. In our opinion no guest will mind sharing a room with the homeowner's hobbies or business work space. We do recommend though that you keep this type of activity contained to its own corner or half of the room. When you have a guest to stay, ensure this area is tidy so that your guest doesn't have to have clutter in their face as they try to get to sleep.

A guest room with floor to ceiling wardrobes is ideal for extra storage space. And a great storage system for shoes can be a floor to ceiling cupboard tucked into a corner behind the door with multiple fitted shelves each just high enough to take a row of shoes so you can have multi layers of shoes neatly organized and all clearly visible and easy to access.

More Tips

Organizing accessories

Women definitely have a multitude of items in this category, and here are a few ideas which we recommend:

- Necklaces and bracelets can be pinned to a cork board which in turn can be hung on the back of a door or in a discrete corner of the bedroom.
- Scarves can be hung on a hook on the back of a door, or folded with some scented sachets in a pretty decorative box.
- Handbags hang beautifully on a coat/hat stand which keeps them in shape and creates an attractive display.

- Belts can be hung from hooks inside the wardrobe door.

Sports gear

Gear such as scuba equipment which you may use in Summer months, ski gear for Winter, and all year round bike gear, can be stored in a cupboard in the garage.

Tall narrow cupboards don't take up much space, can slot into a corner of a garage, and a cupboard such as this dedicated to sports gear would put paid to those harassed searches through the whole house for tennis balls, bike riding gloves and helmet, or your goggles. A shelf in the cupboard could be dedicated to each person's gear, or you could organize each shelf relative to a specific sport or activity.

Luggage

Where possible stow smaller pieces of luggage inside larger suitcases, and if you have room, store these on top of the wardrobe, under beds, or in a cupboard in the garage.

Luggage that you don't use very often can also be useful for storing out of season clothes and shoes (pop shoes in bags or wrap them in old pillow cases in case there's any residue of dirt on the soles).

Mirrors

Feng Shui experts advise that you shouldn't have a bedroom mirror positioned so that you can see your own reflection from your bed; and mirrors in a bedroom can also adversely affect your sleep.

These experts also advise not to have mirrors in children's bedrooms at all, unless they particularly request one. If your child wants a mirror in their bedroom you could perhaps hang it on an inside wardrobe door.

Mirrors however can be ideal for opening up a space and creating the illusion of a small room looking larger. We would use these tactics in other rooms though rather than in bedrooms.

Using the back of doors for hanging systems

The idea here is to cleverly use the back of a door to hang items, without having it look cluttered. You can buy single hooks, or a set of several hooks, which can either be attached to the back of a door, or slot over the top of the door.

While we would not suggest that you use this as a place to hang clothes, this is somewhere you could hang your bathrobe, nightgown, or long flowing scarves or hats.

If you keep your bedroom door open, you can always hang your mirror on the back of the door which has it available without being in plain view.

Archiving clothes

Angella always archives her out of season clothes and shoes so that her wardrobe remains uncluttered. Heavy winter clothing takes up a lot of room in a wardrobe and doesn't need to be there in summer months. Wrap winter shoes and boots and store them away too.

You can use either a suitcase, or storage containers which will slip under beds. Types of containers that will fit under the bed are various, for example the long narrow type of plastic storage container, or canvas storage bags which are ideal for clothes and linen.

What to discard from your wardrobe

We've mentioned sorting your clothes by season, but this is another subject entirely. This is about giving away clothes that you absolutely don't wear.

Angella is not an advocate of giving away clothes just because you may not have worn an item for six months or a year. She has often resurrected something from the back of her wardrobe not worn for a year or two which has now come into its own—maybe a new top goes perfectly with that five year old skirt; or you suddenly have a hankering to wear that beautiful suit you haven't worn for a couple of years.

What you do want to discard is:

- Any clothes that are a size or more too small, or too large. If you are holding onto clothes which you no longer fit, every time you look at them you're going to beat yourself up because you've put on weight. And if some items are a size or two larger than what you are now, don't hold onto them because 'you might put that weight back on'—you're setting yourself up here too.
- An item of clothing which you've tried on several times and it just never seems to look right so you take it off every time.
- If the color doesn't do you justice—you know when you put something on whether you look in the peak of health, or whether you look like you're on your way to hospital with a bout of jaundice.
- If you're holding onto that dress/coat/suit that sister or aunt gave you and which you never really loved anyway. Don't feel obligated to keep something just because someone gave it to you.
- The bottom line here is, only keep in your wardrobe what fits, what looks good, and what you love.

Give away toys, books etc

Every child is bound to still have old toys and books which they no longer treasure or play with. Ask their permission first and then suggest that they might like to donate them to a local charity or children's hospital. You can also explain that when their room is full of toys and books they no longer want, there's no room for any new stuff.

Angella's niece's solution with her young boys was to tell them that if they put their toys and books that they no longer wanted on Trade Me they would get to keep the proceeds. One bought himself an IPOD with what he earned from selling his toys, and the other saved his dollars earned to put towards something special later on.

Hoarding

We really suggest you don't hoard your babies' clothes and gear unless you're expecting another baby sometime in the future. It's a fact that many mothers feel attached to their baby's first wee outfit and darling little shoes baby first wore, and it's lovely to keep these items so we're not suggesting these are the things you pass on. However, one of Angella's clients kept absolutely everything from her child's birth onwards, which included a baby car seat (and her baby is now a grown up).

There will always be someone who would love to have some previously loved baby clothes, cot and car seat, so why not pass them on to willing hands.

Overview—Angella's Laws

Safety

- Beware of electrical appliances in bedrooms: tie up cables and cords, don't have long extension cords that run across rooms which can become a tripping hazard (these can be tacked to architraves near the carpet line).
- Don't overload electric power points.
- Ensure heaters in bedrooms are safe, and can't be easily knocked over by a running child.
- Ideally everything should come off the floor and be put in its own space on shelves, in cupboards or in storage boxes, to allow the room to be cleaned and aired regularly.
- Dust accumulated in hard to get to corners and cluttered areas can encourage crawling insects, and may also cause or aggravate allergies.
- Toys scattered all over the floor can create a hazard for little bare feet, and potential choking danger for wee toddlers who crawl into big brother or sister's bedroom.
- Good lighting and lamps in bedrooms where the occupants are reading, or doing homework, are important to save from future eye strain.
- Safety locks on windows are a good idea not only to stop outsiders getting in, but also to stop toddlers from leaning out and falling.

And practicality

- Educate the family to return items to their place when used.
- Think twice about using white or light colored carpet, or furnishings, in children's bedrooms.
- Kids change so fast and outgrow fads so it's often better to keep color schemes simple rather than buy expensive fad-specific wallpaper.

- Bright colored storage boxes look good as well as being functional.
- Keep everything off the floor—put a laundry basket in kids' rooms so dirty clothes are not mixed up on the floor with clean clothes.
- Don't hoard baby or children's clothes or gear—give it away (unless you're keeping it for the next baby).
- Don't allow anything in a bedroom that doesn't belong—keep rooms specific.

Questions & Answers

Q **We have two daughters who live in our three-bedroom home. My husband and I share the large master bedroom and our elder girl has the next bedroom which is a reasonable size. The third bedroom is only a box room and far smaller than the other two. Charlotte who lives there is complaining that it's too small for her and she ought to get her sister's room when Lucy goes to university next year. This is causing tension between the two of them.**

A One of the great things about living in a house like yours is that although the third bedroom might be tiny it has a high ceiling and it occurs to us that you could build a high sleeping platform which would free up loads of room below. Peter built what was in effect a huge shelf across his younger daughter's bedroom and installed a small sofa and wardrobe space below. The room seemed a lot larger and greatly impressed Emma's mates.

Q **The layout of our house is pretty unusual. The open plan kitchen and lounge is on the first floor, we use the ground floor as a study and a craft room cum second study, and the basement houses the bathroom and the master bedroom. Anyone wishing to use the bathroom walks down some stairs and can look through a window into our bedroom. It's more a minor irritant than a major problem but we'd rather not have people checking out the most intimate room in the house. Curtains would look a bit twee and would cut down on the little natural light we already have. Help.**

A We would suggest that you replace the clear (normal) glass in the window with opaque glass that allows light to pass through but makes it impossible for people to see through. You can either replace the glass or cover existing glass with a film of opaque covering which you can buy from a glazier.

Putting it on can be tricky as it dries quickly and you can be left with unsightly bubbles. What you need to do is clean the glass with methylated sprits to remove grease and grime, then spray with water, a small plant sprayer will do, before removing the backing paper and carefully applying the opaque covering to the glass.

The best way to remove bubbles is by smoothing them out using an old plastic credit card. This covering is not cheap but is less hassle than replacing the glass.

Q **Help—I love having friends and family come to stay and they all say my guest room is such a lovely inviting room. However, I sometimes find that guests can tend to outstay their welcome—it's a bit like that Chinese proverb that says guests are like fish and they go off after two or three days. How do you suggest I gently get them to move on?**

A This is often a tricky situation as we don't want to offend friends or family by asking them to leave after a few days. Of course if you are using your guest room for other purposes, such as a home office, craft room or study room for the kids, then overstayers will soon see that it's not very convenient for them to stay too long in a room that you need to be able to access on a regular basis.

Conclusion

Have some fun with these exercises, they can become part of your planning process. You can use this space, or use a notebook if you prefer.

1. What would your ideal master bedroom look like, and what would you have to do to achieve it?

_____

_____

_____

_____

_____

_____

2. How do you think you can get buy-in from the other people in your house to create and maintain their rooms as areas they'll enjoy into the future?

_____

_____

_____

_____

_____

_____

3. List some of the desirable items you'd like to buy for each bedroom
    and add them to your planning process.

    _____

    _____

    _____

    _____

    _____

    _____

Chapter Six

Dining and Living Areas

Our dining and living rooms are the main family rooms of the home, where we enjoy time spent together. The dining area is where we share meals with family and friends, while the living area is where we relax at the end of a long day, settle in front of the TV, and play with the kids before bedtime. We therefore want these rooms to be inviting, warm and welcoming where we can experience that sense of comfort and family enjoyment.

In some homes dining and living areas will be separate rooms. The dining room may be reserved primarily for formal entertaining with a separate eating area in the kitchen catering for the many comings and goings of a busy family. These rooms were often the hub of any home where multi-generational members of a family got together for the classic Sunday roast. Now we all live such busy lives that more often than not mum and dad and the teenagers see each other on the fly and rarely actually sit down to eat together.

In many contemporary homes dining and living areas are combined in a large open plan format. These areas may be well defined with different color or decorative finishes, or they may subtly blend into each other.

However our family areas are configured in our home, it's important that these areas nurture and envelop us into the warmth that is family.

Of course, given the very nature of these rooms which are often multi-functional, they can quickly become chaotic. Dining rooms become a space to do homework, work on that project on the dining table, and yet another play area for little ones, as well as serving family as a place to meet for meals. Living rooms are a place to relax and listen to music or watch TV and DVDs, where we entertain guests, and again where kids often play. Oops, does that sound repetitive? Yep, we've found that kids tend to drag their toys into every room in the house, including the bathroom and toilet . . .

We're combining our decluttering ideas for dining and living areas in this chapter as they logically go together and also both areas often suffer from the same problems.

So let's begin our four step process:

- Assessment
- Planning
- Implementation
- Evaluation

Assessment

Stand back and honestly assess your dining and living areas, and ask yourself these questions, and any others that pop into your mind:

- How cluttered is your dining area? Do you have to move objects from the table and/or chairs before you sit down to eat?

105

- Is it easy to just sit down at the table for a meal or do you have to hunt and find chairs which are also being used in other rooms?
- Is your dining area small and so crammed with furniture that you have to breathe in as you sit at the table?
- Are you able to really relax in your living room without being distracted by a multitude of objects and papers on top of furniture and all over the floor?
- Are your sofa and comfy chairs in the right position to provide a conversation area, as well as having a good view of the TV?
- Do you have tables beside the sofa for your coffee or glass of wine?
- Do you knock your shins on the coffee table in front of the couch every time you walk past it?
- Do you have an entertainment unit for your TV and related systems, including storage of DVDs and CDs, or are they piled on top of each other with electrical leads spilling out all over the floor?
- Do you have a book case or shelves for favorite books?
- Is there a pile of paper clutter such as newspapers, magazines, periodicals, and work papers that never seems to get cleared away?
- Have the children's toys and books found their way into the area, and now live there permanently?
- Do pets tend to scatter the floor with leaves and twigs from the garden and lawn?
- Do you bring the laundry in and leave it unfolded on the sofa and chairs until you can get to it?
- Have the sofa and chairs, or dining area, become a dumping ground for the kids' jackets and school things when they get home from school?

As you're making your notes, don't forget to write down anything about these rooms that really frustrates you and that you'd like to see changed. A room can be simply transformed sometimes by shifting just one piece of furniture, and clearing the clutter.

Plan

The Planning process will take into account everything you've written down that's not working, as well as your desired outcomes. Now that you have a clear picture of what's not working, decide where you're going to start.

So write down on your plan to tackle one area at a time, and tick tasks off as you do them. This way you'll start to see everything fall into place. And keep in mind how you'd like to see the room—what is your ideal: minimalist, cozy, chic?

Implement

As we've said in previous chapters, create enough uninterrupted time to allow you to get really stuck in. Decluttering and reorganizing a room can take a few hours, and particularly in this case as you may be looking at two areas, so you may even want to plan on taking two or three bites at it.

When Angella is working with a client on a very cluttered area they will often do it over two appointments, not only for the time factor but also because it can be quite tiring, especially when moving furniture and heavy objects. However, ultimately it's extremely satisfying and the end result is so worth the effort. Once systems are in place it becomes a simple matter to keep them maintained.

Evaluate

The evaluation process is also important as you're working on your plan, as what you might have decided would work on paper may not be so convenient in actuality.

Therefore as you declutter, clear and reorganize, do take a minute to check that placement of furniture and objects is ideal for day to day living.

And once you've finished, evaluate again after a few days of using the rooms so you can assess what could be tweaked to work even better.

Practical Steps to Declutter your Dining Room and Living Room

Start with one area and focus on just that area. In other words, don't look at your large open plan dining/living area and think "oh heavens, how am I going to do all this?" Pick the smaller area, which will usually be the dining section, and as you see that room come together you will be spurred on to do the next.

Dining Table and Chairs

Now this may seem obvious, but a cluttered table and chairs with clothes hanging over them will not be conducive to relaxed dining. This may be the first place you start—take everything off the dining table, and chairs, and sort it as you go. These items will often be children's clothing, papers, books, and such like. As you are working through the various rooms of your house with this book you may have already sorted spaces for books and papers. And of course the children's items go back to their bedrooms.

Draping clothes over the back of chairs is merely a habit and anyone in the house can be re-educated to take their belongings to their room. Angella remembers the frustration with her Italian flatmate many years ago when she was living in Rome, as he would fling his jackets over the back of the dining chairs as soon as he entered the house. She managed to break him of this habit by picking up his garments each time he laid them over a chair and dropping them on the floor. That may seem harsh although it wasn't done in anger, but with some amusement; he soon discovered that it was just as easy to take his jacket to his room.

If you tend to work on the family accounts at the dining table, keep a file or archive box alongside you so that after each working session you can put everything into the file or box and return it to the area of your house that you've designated as an admin or home office zone. The beauty of using a box is that everything including the cheque book, pens and calculator, can be tucked in with the accounts, and the lid closed so it's all contained in the one area.

Cupboards & Drawers in the Dining Room

If you have a sideboard, dresser, or cupboard in your dining room you may have already found that this is ideal for storing china, cutlery and serving plates. And there may also be room for good crystal glassware, and a drinks cabinet. In effect you are setting up this area for 'entertaining' dinnerware, when you put plates on the table and let guests serve themselves. Drawers in a dining room cabinet or cupboard are also handy to store your good canteen of cutlery, and special placemats and serviettes.

The usual china and cutlery which you use for everyday family meals would continue to reside in the kitchen.

Shelves in the Living Room

Book shelves or a book case are perfect in a living room where you are most inclined to relax with a good book. If you have children in your household, you may wish to dedicate an area of the book case to them for their special books.

It's also useful to categorize your books so they're easy to find; some people stack their books by author while others group them by type. This is a great time saving trick.

Most of us have some precious decorative ornaments which we like to keep on display and if you have empty shelves you can create a lovely effect. We're not opting for a minimalistic approach here, it's more by way of keeping clutter at bay and unnecessary items in their place.

If you're an avid collector, why not display your fabulous collection on shelves, or inside cubes appended to the wall. Collections create visual impact and can become a lovely point of interest in a fairly plain living area.

Cupboards may contain many articles, ranging from games, books, and a mix of objects which seem to live in this area because you can't figure out a better place for them. Do group like objects together, so whatever you have in the cupboard, store logical items on the same shelf. This is also a good time to declutter these cupboards as more often than not there will be items which could be better stored elsewhere.

Coffee Tables

These are classic junk gatherers including old magazines, unopened mail, newspapers etc. Nothing will make a living area look cluttered like lots of paper and miscellaneous objects scattered over every available surface.

Coffee tables have a specific purpose i.e. a place to set down your cup of coffee or glass of wine which is handy to where you're sitting.

While TV remotes usually take pride of place on coffee tables, some side tables have a drawer to house these objects. If you're ready to buy a new coffee table or two, do get one with at least one drawer, or shelves, so you can tuck away as much as possible. You'll notice a difference even by just clearing the top of the coffee table.

Entertainment Unit

Entertainment units generally incorporate the TV, DVD player and music system, and include storage space for CDs and DVDs.

A piece of furniture which serves to contain all of these items together is the optimum, or it may be a designated cupboard or shelf unit which will also house CDs and DVDs.

Or it may be that you have a small cabinet on which sits the TV with the other equipment inside the cabinet. If this is the case, you can store CDs and DVDs in attractive boxes and sit the boxes alongside the TV cabinet. Stack the CDs / DVDs on their side so you can read the spine without having to pull everything out to find the one you want.

Storage

Baskets and/or decorative storage boxes are useful solutions for all sorts of items which normally live in dining and living areas. For example, if you don't have a cupboard or drawers in your dining area, and there's no room in the kitchen, you can use decorative boxes for any number of items, such as:

- Miscellaneous items for entertaining such as serviettes and napkin rings, and special items which you may use to decorate the table when entertaining.
- Candles, candle holders and matches or lighters.
- Household accounts with cheque book, pens and stapler etc (if these don't live in the home office space).
- Magazines and periodicals—once the box or basket becomes full, throw out the older issues.
- A small basket alongside a sofa can be used for remote controls.

If you're using fancy boxes then they can stack neatly on top of each other and become a feature in a corner of the room, or even slide unobtrusively under a coffee table.

More Tips

- Magazine containers are attractive and can sit neatly alongside a couch or armchair. Cull them regularly so you're only holding on to those which are most recent.
- Ottomans often come with storage inside them—these are so useful for games, or magazines and books. The idea is to have your objects at hand, but not in full view.
- Use walls for your displays rather than table tops, but don't clutter the walls otherwise the room will look too busy.
- Wall units or cubes attached to a wall effectively display your precious items, beautiful vases and figurines, and favorite photos.
- If your dining or living area is quite small, think about using glass coffee and dining tables. Glass furniture doesn't close in a room as large wooden tables tend to do.

Overview—Angella's Laws

Safety

- Ensure that placement of furniture does not impede movement in a room, or cause tripping or falling.
- Sharp edges on furniture, particularly coffee tables, can cause nasty scrapes so again check that there is plenty of room to move around the furniture.
- If bringing hot plates into the dining area from the kitchen, have a place to set them down, such as a sideboard, if not placing them directly on the table.
- Hot coffee cups placed on cluttered side tables are also a hazard waiting to happen, especially if young children are running around.
- Make sure heaters are in a place where children can't inadvertently bump into them.
- Tie up TV and electric equipment cords and ensure power points are safe.

And practicality

- Think 'uncluttered' areas, and keep surfaces of furniture clear of anything that absolutely doesn't need to be there.
- Create good habits around returning objects to their 'home' after each use.
- If you decide you don't need certain pieces of furniture in these rooms, think about where else they could be utilized e.g. a sideboard could be relegated to the garage for a gardening table, library area, or a workbench.
- You can use decorative boxes for storage of objects such as CDs and DVDs, work papers and bills, and games.
- Furniture that doubles as storage is useful, e.g. coffee tables with shelves or cubby holes to store current magazines and books, or a chest which can double as a coffee table and also contain games and books. Oftentimes one piece of furniture can do the work of two.

Questions & Answers

Q My children use the dining room table for their homework, and my husband uses it for his work papers and paying the bills. And they all leave it in an absolute mess so I have to clear everything off the table before I can set it for dinner. How can I keep them off the dining table, or at least get them to clear it off when they've finished?

A Is there enough space in the kids' rooms for a table or small desk where they could do their homework? If not, tell them when they've finished they have to clear the table completely and put all of their stuff in their bedroom.

Get a box to contain work papers and household bills, put some plastic sleeves or files inside the box so hubby can sort his papers. That way when he's ready to do the accounts he can just pick up the box, bring it out to the dining room to work on it (if he doesn't have a home office area), and when he's finished it all goes back inside the box which can reside on a shelf, inside a wardrobe, or under a table.

If you then get a beautiful vase of flowers and place it bang in the middle of the dining room table, it can be moved to one side when they're working on the table, but you can tell them that the vase has to go back to the middle of the table when they've finished.

Q The living room is so cluttered and messy that I would be ashamed to invite anyone in for a drink. The laundry gets dumped there after getting it in from the line, newspapers build up in one corner together with old magazines, and the kids' toys are scattered everywhere. I can't seem to see beyond the mess to even begin to organize the room.

A Family living areas do get cluttered very easily, but if you can put a few systems in place, and then educate the family as to where everything goes, you've got a better chance of keeping a modicum of harmony in the room.

First, clear everything off furniture surfaces (this is a major rule when it comes to decluttering), decide what needs to go and what can stay then find places for everything.

Papers can go into files or boxes, newspapers go into recycling, magazines can be put into a magazine stand. Once you're decluttered the kids' rooms they will know where their toys go—give them an incentive if necessary (we hesitate to call it a bribe) to put their toys away at the end of the day, and they'll soon learn good habits as they discover how much easier it is to find a particular toy if they've put it away in its proper place.

The best way to handle laundry is to fold it directly from the line (or clothes dryer) and stack it in a laundry basket or hamper for ironing. What doesn't need ironing can be sorted and go in everyone's rooms to be put away in drawers. If you put it away straight after it comes off the line, you'll be saving yourself the annoyance of having it hanging around and making you feel guilty every time you see it cluttering the room.

Q **Talk about clutter! The book shelves in the living room have become a place where everyone dumps CDs, DVDs, toys, comics and newspapers. It's driving me mad. We love our books but everything else has taken over. And don't even talk about the side tables beside the sofa—they're piled high and there's barely room for a coffee cup.**

A Any flat surface or shelf becomes a candidate for dumping! We suggest you clear everything off the book shelves and only put back your books. Everything else gets relocated: old newspapers can go in the recycle bin; CDs and DVDs can be sorted into matching decorative storage boxes which can sit on top of each other alongside the TV; kids' toys and comics go into containers in their bedrooms—teach them where everything goes so they can put their own stuff away. Even little kids can learn good habits. Side tables beside the sofa are ideally just for the coffee cup, or wine glass, TV remotes, and your book. Everything else goes.

Once you declutter all of the surfaces of your furniture, you may have to go through a little trial period with the family to make sure they understand that this is now a system and for the ease and comfort of you all as a family, you want them to use the system.

Q I've just moved into a very small apartment with open plan dining room/lounge combined. How can I make best use of the space with my furniture so I can define the different areas?

A Small apartments especially need to be kept clutter-free as you'll quickly run out of room otherwise. The furniture you use in your combined dining room/lounge will enable you to delineate the two areas. Basically you can divide the room in half so it's clear which is your dining area and which is your lounge.

Ideally you don't want too much furniture in your dining area, and you may wish to consider a glass dining table as this will keep the room lighter and less closed in. You can define your lounge area by placing your sofas in a conversational half circle, and even place the back of a sofa to the dining area if this works. Or place the sofas along the opposite walls in the lounge half of the room and place a small coffee table at the end of each sofa so the coffee tables in effect will demarcate the beginning of the lounge area. Another way to divide the two areas is with a tall pot plant or two, strategically placed where you're not going to bump into them, although this will depend on the amount of space you have in the overall room.

Use decorative storage boxes for your bits and pieces—these come in different sizes from small to large and can sit on top of each other so they're space savers and at the same time create a pretty display in an unused corner.

And don't forget, try to maintain clear uncluttered surfaces as much as possible. One or two objects on the dining table, and maybe an item or two on coffee tables will stop the room from looking too minimalist while enabling you to show off some pretty pottery or display pieces.

Conclusion

You might like to use these exercises as part of your planning process. Use an exercise book if you prefer.

1. What's the type of look you'd love to create in your dining and living areas? Is it elegant and chic, country charm, or contemporary casual?

    _____

    _____

    _____

    _____

    _____

    _____

2. Think of creative ways you can set up new habits for the family to continue to maintain the rooms post-decluttering.

    _____

    _____

    _____

    _____

    _____

    _____

3. Write down your 'wish list' for these rooms whether it's new furniture, new drapes or some beautiful paintings to hang on the walls.

_____

_____

_____

_____

_____

_____

CHAPTER SEVEN

BATHROOM, LAUNDRY & LINEN

Y our bathroom, utility room and linen cupboard are as likely to collect clutter as anywhere else in your home. And, as elsewhere, a multitude of miscellaneous items not only reduces the usefulness of these areas but can also make these rooms an eyesore.

If you stop and think about them, bathrooms serve a number of different functions. The quick shower before an even quicker weekday breakfast has a different feel to a slow Sunday soak used to sooth away those physical and psychological strains that we subject our bodies and minds to. A bathroom is a place where we can be truly alone, where we can sing, think and solve problems. Solutions to difficulties that you have been worrying about are more likely to surface while soaping yourself in a shower or shaving than anywhere else, with the possible exception of the bedroom. Time spent in this room can be special but a cluttered environment can detract from our enjoyment.

Where once there was only soap and shampoo there is now a staggering array of specialist products: face cleansers, body washes, facial scrubs, pre-shave balms and much more, and that's just for the man in the house.

Throw in the stuff our dentists expect us to use such as floss and solutions, boxes of contact lenses, things for our nails, creams to remove unwanted hair and products to improve the hair we want to keep, you soon sense that this stuff needs to be organized so you can find it easily when you need it.

And while products we no longer use might not take up a lot of space on their own, they need to be culled ruthlessly so that we don't grab for the earwax remover instead of the tea tree oil.

Whether it's a quick wash before hurrying off to work or a leisurely session at the weekend, well organized storage of all these toiletries reduces stress. Hunting for a nail file or tweezers is frustrating, as well as being an utter waste of time. Clutter a basin with any of the aforementioned products and sooner or later something is bound to slip into the water. It also goes without saying that crowded worktops take longer to wipe down and keep clean.

And then there's the first aid supplies which need to be stored safely, but still within easy reach so you're not hopping on one foot trying to staunch the blood while desperately hunting down bandages and antiseptic cream. This is an area which can easily become cluttered with expired medicines, tablets and such like and needs to be regularly assessed.

Whether you store linen in your bathroom, or in a room that houses a washing machine and tumble dryer, there is a danger that space for things that you actually use is choked up with old bath towels, duvet covers and bedspreads that have long ended their useful life, at least in your home. Keep this redundant stuff and sooner or later this storage space will be insufficient and things you need will migrate elsewhere.

Bathrooms, laundry rooms and linen cupboards are three areas that are sometimes inter-related and in smaller homes sometimes sharing the same space. For this reason there can be a fair bit of overflow from one area to another creating havoc once you add the family's many bathroom items, coupled with steeped high laundry baskets, and stacks of linen.

We'll deal with each area separately, and look at how to cope with overlapping areas, such as when we have a washing machine nestled into a corner of a small bathroom, and a linen cupboard which may well be located in the bathroom.

Bathrooms need to be not only functional with their primary use being bathing, toileting and grooming, they also need storage areas for a wide assortment of items. Whether our bathroom is a shared family bathroom, or an ensuite off the master bedroom, it will always benefit from being well organized.

So where do we start?

Using our same format as in the other chapters, we'll go through the following steps:

- Assessment
- Planning

- Implementation
- Evaluation

Assessment

Stand back in the doorway of your bathroom, and scan the area objectively. Ask yourself a series of questions such as these outlined below to get clarity on what's working, and what's definitely not working for you in this area of your home.

- Does the bathroom feel like mayhem in the mornings as everyone tries to get ready at once?
- Is your bathroom multi-functional, having to double also as the laundry?
- Do you have adequate storage space?
- Do you need more shelving, or cupboards?
- Is the vanity unit packed to overflowing with the whole family's assorted items?
- What's in the bathroom that absolutely doesn't need to be there?
- What are your frustrations?
- Is the room properly ventilated or does it tend to stay damp?
- Are there toxic substances that a child or pet could swallow?
- Is this where you keep your medicines and if so, are they easily accessible and safely stored?

Planning

Once you've got an idea of what needs to be done in the bathroom, write out your plan:

- Think about the other people sharing the bathroom and their needs—if they have a dedicated area for their particular items then they'll be more inclined to keep their area organized.

- Consider the safety aspects mentioned at the end of this chapter, and factor them into your planning.
- Map out the area/s where there's space for additional shelves, a cupboard or some baskets for storage.
- Decide what can be taken out of the bathroom and stored in a more appropriate room of the house (if it's unrelated to the bathroom move it somewhere else).
- If you keep your medicines in the bathroom, create a dedicated area or cupboard where these can be contained safely.
- If your bathroom contains a washing machine/dryer there may be a way you can section it off, say with a standing screen or even a curtain so the two areas become more defined, or the surface of the appliances may be used to hold laundry baskets or spare towels.

Implementation

Now you've created your plan, it's time to set aside an uninterrupted hour or two to work through your ideas. If you've decided on more shelving, have them put up before you start the process so everything is in place for you when you're ready to get going. Make sure you have a rubbish bag or two so you can get rid of expired medicines, creams and lotions as you work.

Evaluation

Stand back and assess what you've done. Picture all members of the household and how they use the bathroom, are they are naturally messy individuals who need ultra-organized systems to keep their belongings contained, or do your small children scatter their toys all over the floor and inside the bathtub.

Now that you've decluttered and organized the bathroom you need to educate the family as to where everything is kept—check with them that your systems make sense to them as well as to you. We all think differently and what may be logical to one person may not be to another.

As you use the room over the next few days you'll soon see any systems which may need tweaking.

Practical Steps to organize your bathroom

As with other rooms, organization starts with a systematic inspection of what you have. Cupboards and shelves need to be emptied and inspected. You might find it helpful to remove the lot to a kitchen table where, with a black plastic sack at the ready, you should ask yourself these questions:

- What is it?
- Does anyone living here still use it?
- Has the use by date expired?
- Do I (we) need to keep it?
- If yes, does it belong in the bathroom or is it better kept elsewhere?
- If no, should it be given or thrown away?

Bathroom Storage

Typically a traditional pedestal basin has made way for a fitted sink that is built into a vanity unit. Doors open to reveal a large space divided by one shelf. This type of cupboard is pretty much a recipe for clutter. With no dividers provided to define areas, it soon becomes impossible to find anything.

There are numerous options to help you keep makeup, toiletries and medicines separate and easy to find and it is not difficult to improvise using simple plastic containers or boxes in a similar way that we used them in kitchen drawers. How these varied items are sorted will depend on the number of occupants using the bathroom, and whether the items are owned and used by everyone or belong to an individual.

For example, sunscreen, insect repellent and toothpaste will generally be used by everyone so may go together in one or two containers designated for family use.

Each family member will usually also have their own bathroom products, and this will include children who have their favorite bubble bath, skin care lotion and shampoo.

Use separate containers of products for each person so that each container is immediately identifiable to its owner. Keep in mind that you want to be able to slide each container in and out of the cupboard so items are easy to reach.

This system also means each person is responsible for putting their own things back into their container, which in time will hopefully become a habit and therefore put a stop to the array of items congregating on the basin top.

Another example may be the more modern bathroom with a multi-drawer cabinet beneath the basin, so each drawer can be designated with a particular function. You can decide whether your storage cabinet or drawers are sorted by function, or by person.

Spare stock items like extra rolls of toilet paper or bars of soap can be kept in a different place than products that are currently in use, for example on a laundry shelf or cupboard.

Another useful item in a bathroom is a laundry hamper for used towels. If you have room in your bathroom for something like this it can be a blessing. It becomes easy for family members to dump their wet towels in the hamper rather than leaving them scattered all over the floor, or draped over the bath.

As with other areas of the home, storage boxes can also be used in the bathroom, and are both decorative and practical. Or you could try a slim-line shelving stand which could fit neatly into a corner and used for miscellaneous objects such as towels, shampoos, soaps and lotions. Another option is a standalone unit with drawers, which is on wheels so you can move it easily from one position to another if necessary. All of these options can work wonderfully fulfilling the vital role of storage and looking good at the same time.

Shower and bath caddies are also extremely useful and there's a vast array of designs to choose from. It is definitely more practical, and safer, to have your soap and shampoo products appended at eye level in the shower cabinet, rather than on the floor which will necessitate bending, and potentially slipping.

A shower seat or stool can be a great idea, and isn't just for the aged and slightly infirm. You can sit back and enjoy the jets of water over your body, or use the stool to prop your foot up for leg-shaving purposes.

Another clever idea for organizing your bathtub accessories is to hang them with hooks onto a couple of towel rails affixed to the wall above the bath. It can create a quirky feature on an otherwise bare wall. And a shoe pocket container can be hung on the back of the bathroom door for hair dryers, brushes and other miscellaneous objects.

Even the kids' bath toys can be taken care of and kept contained either using a plastic container which hooks onto the sides of the bath; or you could use suction caps to suspend a large firm plastic pouch from the wall above the bath.

And above all, we really feel that bath time can quite delightful, so why not lie back and enjoy. A wooden tray hooked to each side of the bath will securely hold a glass of wine and a snack, and some of these trays even include a book stand! What more could you wish for.

As we mentioned earlier in this chapter, your bathroom can also serve as a sanctuary. So why not create this as one of your favorite areas in your home.

Beautifying your bathroom may be as simple as placing a vase of flowers on a ledge, or using beautiful containers for makeup items. Adorn the walls with some framed artwork; and glass shelves look lovely with a few objects well placed such as gorgeous perfume bottles.

The Laundry

When your laundry appliances are located within your bathroom, it's ideal if they can be stacked on top of each other thereby saving as much space as possible. The main thing is that these appliances don't dominate the entire bathroom.

You can create storage solutions for laundry detergents which may be as simple as some attractive wicker baskets, with lids, which will tuck alongside or on top of the machine/s.

Standalone Laundry Rooms

You may be fortunate enough to have a lovely spacious room housing washing machine, dryer, and ample shelving for linen and cleaning products. Alternatively, you may use a custom made wardrobe or cupboard which neatly fits the washing machine and dryer, all tucked away behind bi-fold doors.

The main thing in a laundry room is to have adequate shelving and storage. If your laundry room doesn't have any built in cupboards, then shelves or a freestanding metal shelving rack will work equally as well and can store a variety of items such as:

- Washing detergents
- Household cleaners
- Old cloths, dusters and rags for cleaning
- Sprays
- Peg basket
- Extra toilet rolls and paper products
- Appliances such as iron, dust-buster, and potentially even the vacuum cleaner

Rather than stacking these items directly onto the shelves, we suggest you sort them by category and put them into their own individual containers. It will then be a simple task to find a particular item, and products will ideally stand upright in their container which stops potential spillage.

Tall items, such as ironing board and brooms can stand neatly in a corner of the room, or hang from pegs affixed to the wall.

Larger laundry rooms will potentially also have sufficient space for a clothes rack to hang clothes directly from the dryer, or for drip-drying items. When taking clothes out of the dryer, it's ideal to fold them right away while they're warm—this will save creasing and may even negate the need for ironing. If you don't have room for a permanent table within the space, you may like to get a small fold-away or drop-leaf table to use for folding and stacking clothes.

Laundry Closets

These are often large deep wardrobes which have been cunningly designed to house washing machine and dryer, they're great space savers. It's a simple matter to add some shelves inside the closet, which can be used for the usual laundry detergents, and possibly with space for stacking linen if you don't have a separate linen closet.

Do keep the different cleaning products in containers by category—this will save time. Also if you have plastic containers which stack neatly on the shelves for laundry type products, you can manage any spillage of detergents by simply wiping out the container.

The laundry basket can sit neatly on top of the dryer, and a clothes horse can be hung on a hook on another wall of the closet.

Linen Cupboards

If you have a separate linen cupboard the easiest way to organize it is to sort your linen by category and dedicate a shelf to each type e.g. sheets and pillowcases, duvet covers, towels, face cloths, tea towels etc.

When folding linen, stack towels and sheets with the fold facing towards the front of the cupboard. Besides looking neater, individual items are easier to retrieve.

If you keep sets of bedding together, this also saves time when it's time to change the beds.

Everyday linen should be placed on the most accessible shelves, with blankets and duvets stored on the topmost shelves. If you only have a small linen cupboard, you can use air-compressed bags for out of season linen which will cut down on shelf space needed.

An idea we rather like for linen storage is a wire rack system with shelves in the middle of the unit and supported on each side by a number of wire baskets. You can easily see where everything is stored, and you can still categorize linen into the various baskets. This type of unit could live in a spare bedroom and could double up as temporary storage space for guests coming to stay.

Overview—Angella's Laws

Health & Safety

- Do ensure you have slip resistant mats where necessary i.e. in the bath if you have a shower hose over the bath, and outside the shower cabinet.
- Medicines and dangerous objects such as razor blades should be kept well out of small children's reach and if you keep cleaning products in the bathroom/laundry, make sure these substances are also out of reach of tiny tots.
- Keep appliances with plugs and cords safely in a container or inside a cupboard.
- Ensure good ventilation in the bathroom area so that misting and dampness doesn't create slippery surfaces.
- Make sure any glass in the bathroom is tempered and has no sharp or jagged edges.
- Shower caddies keep shampoos, conditioners and bath gels off the floor which saves slipping and needless spillage.
- Store children's toys in a waterproof container to keep them off the floor of the bathroom and shower stall, these items can cause accidents if they're underfoot.
- Do have at least one towel rail handy to the bathtub and shower stall so you're not stepping out of the bath or shower to retrieve a towel from the other side of the room.

And practicality

- Keep surfaces on your vanity and beside basins as clear of objects as possible.
- If your bathroom cupboard is organized by category and in containers, you'll be able to retrieve items quickly and return them to their place when finished.

- Laundry hampers work well in a corner of the bathroom to capture used towels and dirty clothes.
- Baskets, containers, and wire carts on wheels are good solutions for storing many bathroom and even laundry products.

Questions & Answers

Q **Almost more than anything else I love a long soak in the bath on a Sunday evening. It's the only time in the week when I can relax and let the worries of the world wash over me. Well almost. Trouble is that the other members of the family, my partner Brian and our two kids, leave it looking like a tip: towels and dirty washing on the floor, toothpaste, soap etc scattered over every surface. There are even black tide marks where other members of the family haven't rinsed the bath. So before I can settle down for my lovely long soak I have to spend an age cleaning and tidying the bathroom, which makes me resentful. I don't think I'm unreasonable but everything I have suggested has fallen on deaf ears. Sometimes I think I'm going mad. Help.**

A Other people have described similar difficulties in other parts of the home but it is clear that the more agitated and resentful you become the less you are going to enjoy this special 'me time.' As ever there are a number of different approaches and you can mix and match accordingly. Is your husband aware of how much this situation is getting to you? We're not just talking about a rant at the family just before your bath. Have you spoken to him away from the kids when you have calmed down? Let him know how fed up you are and ask for his support.

You were kind enough to send a snap of what the bathroom looked like before you got to work and while we do sympathize we couldn't help noticing that the storage facilities are at best only perfunctory. You would have trouble getting a large towel on that rail and there doesn't seem enough space to keep everyone's toiletries. Were you to instill a large heated towel hanger and a line of hooks so that everyone can store their own toiletries in those old fashioned toilet bags, the room would be transformed with minimal effort. There are all sorts of perspex organizers on the market that are great for storing make up, cotton wool buds, tweezers and the rest. Call a family meeting to suggest these ideas.

If you make these changes and life reverts to how it was before, we suggest that you go on strike. Go round to your mother's place and have a bath there and have a shower in the en-suite the rest of the time. There's nothing like going on strike to get others to take responsibility.

Hopefully common sense should prevail. Celebrate by getting a candle stick holder attached to the wall so that you can enjoy your soak in this wonderful lighting. And while you're at it why not invest in a supply of those luxurious scented bath balls the size of an orange.

Q   Another gripe I'm afraid. I seem to be taking ages sorting out the dirty washing. We all throw it into a large wicker basket and come washday I have to empty it out on to the floor to sort it into three piles so I can wash whites, colors and delicates separately. I've got a problem with my back so this is definitely not my favorite thing to do, and there has got to be a better way.

A   Your authors have different attitudes to clothes washing and also different solutions. Angella says: "I've got no interest in fussing about with laundry. I use a cold water detergent and wash everything together except anything that has to be hand washed which I do separately. I suggest that you switch over to this powder or liquid and forget about sorting."

Peter says: "I love mindless boring jobs like washing clothes and use this time to think through difficult problems I'm working on. I've never used a cold water detergent but am prepared to stick my neck out and bet it doesn't clean as well as the stuff I use, especially for grubby marks on a white collar. As for white underwear I don't want to go there. My solution is that you get one of those linen containers with two or three compartments and educate the family to put whites and colors in the appropriate compartment. I would also urge parents to get kids involved in using a washing machine at the earliest opportunity, say when they're ten. You can always make it a game to decide what temperature to wash nylon, wool or cotton and show them what happens when you throw in an old pair of white underpants with a new pair of jeans, or how you can shrink an adult's woolen jumper so that it fits a teddy bear if you put it in a hot wash. But make sure that they only do experiments like these under your supervision before they trash something expensive."

Q **We live in a beautiful old villa. We love it a lot and wouldn't want to live anywhere else but it has a damp and cold bathroom that never dries. As you can imagine it's especially bad in winter. We've spoken to our landlord and he isn't much use. He grumbles that it would cost a fortune to get it sorted and hints that he would have to put up the rent to pay for it.**

A Few things are worse than getting out of a warm shower and trying to get dry with a cold damp towel. Then there is all that algae and mildew which looks unsightly and smells awful. A dehumidifier unit in the bathroom will effectively help to get rid of the excessive moisture. This would also help to raise the temperature in the bathroom. Alternatively you could store your towels in another part of the villa and perhaps keep a free standing towel rail in your bedroom so you can just grab a towel off the rail as you move into the bathroom to take your bath or shower.

Conclusion

Please address the following questions as fully as you can. Use an exercise book if you prefer.

1. What would your dream bathroom look like, and how can you work towards creating it in the space you have?

_____

_____

_____

_____

_____

_____

2. What do you hate about your bathroom or laundry? Think of at least 3 ways you could improve the area/s.

_____

_____

_____

_____

_____

_____

3. What systems are you going to set up that the whole family can use to keep the bathroom, laundry and linen areas uncluttered?

_____

_____

_____

_____

_____

_____

CHAPTER EIGHT

GARAGES AND SHEDS

If you think that garages and sheds are the places in a house safe from the clutches of a declutter expert you'd be wrong. While these spaces may remain a chap's citadel, free of female interference, they can be improved by decluttering.

There is an old saying that good fences make good neighbors. It's also a truism that many a solid marriage is based on defined his and her areas of a home. A generalism perhaps, but many men we know defer to their wives when it comes to deciding on the color and design of new curtains for the lounge, the picture that takes pride of place over the hearth and the model of a new washing machine. But many men do so knowing that there is a place or places in the property that will always remain a bloke's bastion even if it's tacked onto the side of the house or parked in the garden. And while there are relationships where practical chores like wallpaper hanging, unblocking drains or gutters and replacing tap washers are done by women, it is more common that the man around the house is usually responsible for these and other practical chores. It therefore makes sense that he takes responsibility for the places where DIY tools and materials are stored along with lawnmowers, gardening equipment and everything else required to manage a mini estate.

Few modern houses have cellars. This is a great pity as Peter can vouch for the advantage of having one of these underground rooms. Back in England he lived in a Victorian terrace house that had a cellar cut out from the chalk the house was built on. It was designed to store coal and had an earthen floor. Over time it proved an ideal workshop and, as it was totally lightproof, was perfect as a photographic darkroom and studio where he could manipulate the studio lights to take stunning monochrome portraits. And when he bought the house next door which had an even bigger cellar that room was a natural home for a half sized snooker table. That cellar later doubled up as a recording studio.

If you are lucky enough to live in a house that does have a cellar, you could use it for any of these purposes or even for cultivating mushrooms, making beer or wine or any one of 101 uses that don't comfortably fit anywhere else. Unless heated, these rooms remain the same temperature all year round which is why they are useful for storing wine as they're the coolest place during a hot summer and the warmest place during a bleak winter.

We're also aware that for some the attraction of a garage or tool shed may be the grime and clutter you so often find there, especially if it is a counterweight to an otherwise over-scrubbed house.

Garages

Apart from Anthony Hopkins, the real star of the classic 2005 New Zealand movie, The World's Fastest Indian, was Burt Munro's garage. Burt built, lived and worked in this place in Invercargill, Southland, working 16 hour days making new parts for his ancient motorbike to prepare it for the many speed records he accumulated as an old aged pensioner.

Garages may primarily be built for cars but, as in Munro's case, most take on additional roles such as workshop, quartermaster's store, home for the chest freezer, washing machine, tumble drier, hose pipes, equipment needed to maintain a garden and possibly a swimming pool. With all of these roles to cope with garages can easily become a dump. As we have stated elsewhere, nothing attracts clutter like clutter. In other words if you allow your garage or shed to become a mess it won't be long before it becomes a dustbin for the whole household. Indeed adult children heading off on their big overseas adventure may also want to contribute things of their own by unloading the contents of a student flat into this space rather than paying for it to go into storage.

Sadly some garages get so crowded that the unfortunate car is banished to the road. Apart from the increased possibility of theft or vandalism, having to leave a car out in all weathers can ultimately create unnecessary wear and tear on the vehicle, and ensures that owners get wet getting to their vehicle when it's raining. And of course this scenario presents a nightmare when struggling with bags of groceries in the rain. If you're fortunate enough to have a garage that you can get to through an inside door, and you work in an office with an underground car park, you can get to and from work without being exposed to the weather. After Angella decluttered Peter's garage it became possible for the first time since he'd lived there to park two cars rather than just one in that space.

As with decluttering any other room you should start with an assessment of the present uses of the space and honestly ask yourself the following questions:

- What is this space being used for now?
- How well is it functioning?
- Is there room for the cars, and kids' bikes?
- Can I find what I need quickly and easily?
- Could this space be used for any other purpose?
- What has it got going for it?
- What are its limitations?
- Does it need re-decorating?

Let's have a look at these questions in turn.

What is this space being used for now?

This might seem an obvious question but as we have already established, garages are flexible spaces and take on different roles. In the absence of a garden shed for instance the garage may become the storage area for garden tables and chairs during winter months along with the barbeque.

It may be the place where camping equipment is kept, or home for an assorted collection of different sizes of bicycles. Some people convert their garage into a home gym with treadmill, bench press, weights and related gear, while others use this space as a kid's rumpus room.

Peter's friend Mike has one of the tidiest garages he has ever seen. Apart from housing his car and a motorbike, there are bookshelves where he keeps his collection of military history books and the walls are covered in photos of aeroplanes that Mike has taken and had enlarged.

How well is it functioning?

Is it easy or difficult to get the car in and out of the garage?

If you decide that the main use of the garage is to house the car, it's worth ensuring that there's adequate parking space. By keeping the floor clear there is less likelihood that you will drive into boxes haphazardly scattered over the floor, and damage your car in the process.

Remember to make allowances so that all the car doors can be opened allowing passengers as well as the driver to get in the vehicle before leaving the garage. Clearly this is not possible in smaller garages.

Can I find what I need quickly and easily?

A good garage storage system makes a huge difference. There are expensive Swedish modular systems on the market that are so versatile that they work equally well in a garage as in a bedroom wardrobe.

Such units take advantage of wall space so that garden brooms, spades and other implements are stored neatly and are easy to see and get to. A good system almost compels you to return a tool to its rightful home once you have finished using it. Off the peg solutions can be expensive as you need to buy individual components but if you have basic carpentry skills you could design and make customized shelving to install on a garage wall.

Angella's use of storage boxes, or plastic containers, applies here as well. You could for example have a storage box or bin devoted to decorating equipment, brushes, rollers and tray, wall papering odds and sods, sandpaper, wood filler and even a dust sheet. Having to only get out one large container when you are about to paint a room means that you can start at once rather than spend a frustrating hour hunting for individual tools and paint brushes. Other containers could hold fishing equipment so that when you next head for the water this container could be put in the car boot and unloaded at the other end.

Tip: **Why not invest in a labeling machine? They are ideal for labeling storage containers when it is not clear what is kept inside. You'll be able to find uses for these machines in almost every room in the house but they're especially useful in garages and sheds.**

Many families accumulate bicycles. Sometimes it seems they breed and produce baby bikes and left alone these machines can take over a garage. However there are all kinds of hooks and brackets for bikes, which can take them off the floor and free up space.

Where and how you store a bike will depend on how frequently it is used. Some people use a bike every day while for others it's once in a blue moon.

Fridges and freezers

Just because you have room in the garage for a fridge or freezer doesn't mean you need one. These white monsters take up a lot more room than their basic dimensions. They have to be clear of the wall and you need enough room to be able to get at them and still open the door.

Ensure that if you do need to store a fridge or freezer in the garage, that you can get at it easily. If you find that you have to open the garage door, reverse the car, open the fridge to get a beer, drive the car back then close the garage door something is wrong.

If the fridge/freezer in the kitchen is big enough for the family consider flogging the one in the garage.

Work benches

A bench with a vice is extremely useful when you are attempting to repair or make something.

In our experience workbenches are even more likely to get cluttered than a kitchen worktop. Ideally you want to get almost everything off the bench, and on the wall or in a tool chest, so that you've got space to work.

Could this space be used for any other purpose?

As we have already noted, garages can be used for any number of functions. Try and stand back and think of your property as a whole.

Moving a home gym to the garage may free up a bedroom for another role—a bedroom perhaps. Like Mike and Bill, you could use part of the garage as a library as well as more conventional uses like a workshop.

If your garage is large enough, you may be able to partition part of it off for a space for your teenagers, a toddler's play area, or even a snooker table and mini bar.

Another thought, if you're a keen gardener, would be to create an area with a bench where you can pot plants and keep all of your gardening tools and implements all together.

What has it got going for it?

One of the reasons that garages are so widely used as workshops is that they have a lot going for them. The large doors and access to a road or driveway means that deliveries can be made directly to the garage door.

A carpenter can take in large sheets of plywood or planks that he could cut down to size; and the garage doors can be left open when furniture is being stripped with acids that give off toxic fumes or something else is being spray painted where you also need to be in a well ventilated space.

What are its limitations?

Some garages, or sheds for that matter, are cold, damp and dark. Some are insecure. By this we do not mean that they have a hang up because they are not a lounge or kitchen, rather that when the door is open contents are on show to passers-by and invite theft. While it is possible to get bottle gas heaters to warm up this room, a cold damp environment is never going to be ideal for storing books or as a potter's workshop.

Work out what limitations this space has for its potential use, and see if it is possible to remedy this limitation. For instance, how much it would cost to install additional lighting, or carpeting say for a gym, and then make an informed decision taking account of the impact this added resource would have on the rest of your property.

Does it need re-decorating?

You may wonder what redecorating has to do with decluttering a garage. We would argue that removing cobwebs and repainting a garage reinforces an overall sense of order and will help you keep this space tidy and organized. The garage may be the first thing you see when you arrive home or the first thing an overseas visitor sees of your home and, as we know, first impressions count. Filling in old screw holes and repainting makes surfaces look clean and attractive. Repainting the garage floor is the sort of thing many people do when they are trying to sell their property at a premier price, but why wait until then. We believe a garage is not just somewhere to dump the car but can be a useful and welcoming room as well.

Sheds

We don't know about you but the word 'shed' conjures up an image of a tiny wooden building in a corner of a garden that is just about big enough to give home to a lawn mower and not much else. But go to one of those places that sells these things and you'll soon realize that there are sheds and sheds. You'll find small ones of course but they will be dwarfed by monster ones with a veranda. They can be positioned to catch the morning or evening sun and Peter once worked in a hospital that had one of these wooden buildings mounted on a large rotating base so it could be repositioned so it could follow the light.

These large structures can be used as a summer house or a home office as they can be insulated to retain heat, and connected to services so that computers, a printer and a fridge can run off mains, a telephone and fax machine linked to the network, and have hot and cold water on tap.

The children's author Roald Dahl wrote from his garden shed for years. He was a tall man and he worked from an armchair and placed a homemade wooden contraption on his lap and it was from this position that he wrote Charlie and the Chocolate Factory, Tales of the Unexpected and much more. During cold weather he put his legs into a sleeping bag to keep them warm. Clearly he could have afforded a plush office but his improvised use of this wooden building served him well and he saw no reason to change.

Dahl is not alone in getting attached to his shed. There are many men who are equally devoted to this particular part of their homes and who go there religiously with serious intent like Mr Dahl, or just to potter around and get away from under the wife's feet.

Making the most of your shed

Reviewing your current usage of a shed is similar to the one suggested for a garage except that you won't have a car to consider. Detached buildings like these that are more often than not made of wood, sometimes become homes for wasps, creepy crawlies or even birds. Timber may be rotten, especially floors, and roofs may become leaky. Doors may not close properly if the building has warped over time so it is worth making an inspection of the building from all angles and perhaps getting a builder to give it the once over as well. Roof felt and plastic guttering can be replaced and a coat of wood preservative can do wonders for the appearance of these buildings. If you are considering upgrading a shed and installing electricity it is worth seeking professional advice as there are dangers in just running an extension lead from the house.

In addition to asking yourself the questions raised about a garage namely:

- What is this space being used for now?
- How well is it functioning?
- Can I find what I need quickly and easily?
- Is there room for the kids' bikes?
- Could this space be used for any other purpose?
- What has it got going for it?
- What are its limitations?
- Does it need re-decorating?

It is worth posing some additional questions like:

- How secure is this building?
- How cold does it get?
- Do I need permission from council to change the use of this building?
- What are the fire risks?
- What are the insurance implications?

Again looking at these bullet points . . .

How secure is this building?

Wooden outbuildings are vulnerable. During a freak hurricane back in 1987 Peter's garden shed was lifted off its base and scattered in next door's garden. Remarkably a builder friend was able to re-assemble it again, but this was the only damage done to the property.

If a shed is housed in a secluded place at the edge of the garden, it can be broken into by the sort of opportunistic thieves who would never dare break into a house. And your neighborhood pyromaniac is more likely to torch your shed than your main dwelling place.

More often than not, sheds contain combustible materials like petrol for the lawn mower or paint stripper, and gas bottles for the barbeque. It can be a good idea to consider how cold the building may become in winter as sub-freezing temperatures damage tins of paint, in which case these would be better stored in the garage.

Decluttering garages and sheds

If you have read through other chapters in this book you will be familiar with the process of decluttering a room. Garages and sheds are no different, except that they are more likely to contain junk that you should have thrown out of the house, but were not quite ruthless enough.

Typically you will rediscover things that you have hung on to just in case they might be of some use at a later date. These might include wood planks and MDF that has been left over from something you made a while back, car seats that your child grew out of a decade ago, the manual lawn mower you didn't get rid of in case the motor mower broke down, and a miscellaneous assortment of rusty screws, bolts and hinges that were salvaged from something discarded long ago. Then there are all those expensive tins of paint with only a dribble left but held onto in case something needed touching up. Open them up and nothing is left under a thick skin. Often there are also broken things like an old TV or something from the kitchen that you haven't quite got round to getting fixed. And not to forget the empty appliance boxes which nobody seems to throw out, just in case they may need them someday.

Discoveries like these are depressing and it is easy to see why so many of us tidy this junk back into neat piles and walk away. But to do so is to limit the function of this room and deprive you of useful space.

As ever get everything out of hidden corners so that it is visible for inspection. Look at each object in turn and honestly ask yourself these questions:

- What's it for?
- Will I, or anyone else in the house, ever use it?
- If needed, how can it be stored so it's found easily?
- If not needed, how should it be disposed of, dumped, given away or even sold?
- If it's broken is it worth mending?

Even for those of us who accumulate and hoard things dumping is oddly liberating. Hand on heart (Peter) has never regretted getting rid of anything.

Incentives help; you might be able to share a friend's skip, or hire one yourself, to dispose of large items that you know you will never find use for. See if you can make up a car load of things that you can give to a charity shop. You could advertise left over floor or wall tiles to anyone willing to pick them up.

Sorting out the wheat from the chaff might be difficult but it is a skill that can be acquired. Once done, the next job is finding new homes for what is left. You may need some storage containers but you should only buy them when you know precisely what you need and where it is going to go. Large plastic storage containers can prevent contents from getting damp and extend their useful life.

Decluttering Steps Summarized

- To get started, take everything out of the garage so you have a clear area to work in. Alternatively, you can begin in one corner and work your way out. Now you can go through the decluttering process described above.

- Decide what else you may use the garage for and define the area e.g. a partitioned area within the garage for a home gym, rumpus room or gardening corner.

- Disassemble or throw out any empty boxes that you're not going to use for storage—they take up far too much room.

- Use clear plastic storage bins with lids for storage in the garage and/or shed, with each storage container having its own designated function, e.g. paint and decorating equipment, sports gear, archived papers and records, household storage. Label each container on the side as to its contents so when the containers are stacked you can read the labels.

- Put brackets on walls for bikes and any other gear that can be hung.

- Hooks can be used to hang wet suits, wet weather jackets, hats etc.

- Clear everything off work benches so you've got space to work on.

- Use a tool board on a wall above your work bench, and tool chests tucked under the work bench.

Overview—Angella's & Peter's Laws

Safety

- Ensure sharp tools and dangerous machines are placed on shelves rather than on the floor where someone can stand or trip on them.
- Use tool chests for storing tools if you're not using a wall system.
- Paint can be toxic so keep it inside a container in a corner of the garage or tool shed.
- Keep any dangerous objects or toxic substances out of the reach of small children.
- Make sure nails aren't left lying on the garage floor where the car is going to be parked, you don't want punctures.

And practicality

- Think 'uncluttered' areas, and keep working areas clear of anything that absolutely doesn't need to be there.
- Once you're decided where everything is to go, return the item to its 'home' after each use.
- Do use clear storage bins for miscellaneous objects and label them on the side so it's easy to see what they contain.
- Use the walls for storing and stacking, keeping the centre of the garage floor clear.
- Stack up the wall, rather than out from it. In other words, use all the available wall space for your storage systems.
- Think also about overhead storage in the garage, this can be useful space for suitcases, fishing rods, and sports equipment.
- If you're using part of the garage for other activities, partition the area off with screens.

Case Study

Bill and Dianne have a lovely big two-storey home which Bill built with loving care. He made sure as he was building that there was a nice big two-car garage with an adjoining room which he had in mind to use as his tool shed. The problem was that the garage rapidly became a dumping ground as tools and machinery vied for space with fishing tackle, rods and hundreds of meters of fishing line—and all of this stuff overflowed from the tool shed into the garage. Needless to say, it wasn't long before there was no room for Bill or Dianne's vehicles. Dianne also wanted some space for extra storage of some of Bill's fishing books, which were still boxed up with nowhere to go. A beer fridge and huge fish freezer were taking up a lot of space, as was Bill's beautiful hand carved table which he was using as a junk repository for grubby tools and machines.

Dianne finally put her foot down and called Angella. They set aside a day and a half, sent Bill off fishing, and got stuck in. Yes, Bill was delighted to leave it all in Angella's hands as he'd already experienced her decluttering abilities in their previous home. As we mentioned in Chapter 2, being a builder and a fisherman, Bill has a huge collection of tools, machinery and fishing paraphernalia. The challenge was to completely reorganize the garage and tool shed so it met both Bill and Dianne's needs, and so that Bill could find things without creating mayhem in the process of his search.

It was decided that Bill's truck didn't need to be garaged, so that left us with half of the garage to play with. That half became Bill's personal area, with his dining sized table as a focal point, completely cleared of all the tools and junk, and the beer fridge moved to a position right behind the chairs so it was nice and easy to reach for a beer when his mates called in. This became a perfect space for Bill to entertain his mates—they didn't need to take off their muddy boots, or even wash their hands. They all love it. Something like this is a magnet for males.

Meanwhile, the tool shed was organized to within an inch of its life, which Angella found fascinating as she tried to work out the use for some of Bill's tools and machines. She and Bill moved a large cupboard which was going spare into his tool room which was used to store specific tools and machinery. His tools were organized by type on the cupboard shelves so it's now easy to see what he has, and find what he's looking for in seconds. A stack of wire baskets was also used for the larger tools and machines.

And on the other side of the garage, still leaving space for Dianne's car, we lined some plastic cubes along the wall, making a nice neat row with the cubes stacked on top of each other, and each cube has its designated use: book storage, gardening tools, gloves and such like, cleaning products, rubbish bags, and gardening hose and attachments.

Bill was bowled over when he walked into the tool shed—his comment was something like "I can actually see everything on the shelves". Considering before the floor was covered with tools and gear there was no way he could even get near the shelves to see what was there, and the cupboard works beautifully as each of the shelves was categorized by item such as: jars of nails, files, nuts and bolts, and a multitude of other interesting gadgets.

Once all of the garage areas had been well defined, it became a simple task to keep items in their own place. And both Bill and Dianne are happy.

Questions & Answers

Q. Over the years I've built up a collection of tools. I seem to spend a lot of time searching for a small screwdriver or drill bit when I need them. Any suggestions?

A   You are not alone, there's many in the same boat. There are a number of possible solutions. You could for example get one of those DIY aprons that tradesmen use that contain lots of pouches for different sized tools so that they can get at something when they are up a ladder and need a hammer, tape measure or anything else for that matter. This is fine if you are carrying out the same sort of jobs but maybe not right for someone who is never sure what job needs doing next.

Another solution would be to construct a tool board. This is one of those large pegboards you see that is painted black where silhouettes of different tools are drawn in a bright color—for some reason yellow is popular—and then brackets, hooks and nails are used to hold individual tools in place.

You can see all the different tools at a glance, and you'll immediately notice which tools are missing. This gives you and other members of the household an incentive to return a tool to its rightful home.

Making a tool board takes time and it is worth the trouble of grouping items when you do create your board. For instance, tool bits need to be near the electric drill, different sized screwdrivers go together, and tools needed for a particular job like a wire brush, scraper and paint brushes needed for decorating live in the same area.

Q. We would like to convert the garage into a rumpus room for the kids. Trouble is that I have a lot of sharp tools and I'm worried that there might be an accident.

A   You are right, garages can be ideal as a children's play area, allowing them somewhere to make a mess, paint and do all sorts of things, especially when it's dark outside or raining. And tools can definitely be dangerous objects in the wrong hands.

Why not invest in the sort of heavy metal tool chests that you find in industrial workshops? They come in all sizes so you should be able to find something that is suitable, or maybe even find something second hand on Trade Me or EBay, or a boot sale, at a fraction of what you'd pay for the same item new.

You could also screen off an area of the garage that you don't want the children getting at with removable screens.

Q Help, the garage has become a dumping ground for our kids who are off overseas and decided we should store their stuff in their absence. There's no room for our own storage needs let alone theirs.

A This is a common problem and Angella admits to having done the same thing to her parents when she moved overseas for a few years. If your kids have a lot of stuff, such as furniture and boxes of belongings, it may be worth your while to invest in an aluminum garden shed which you can put on one side of your property. These sheds are simple to assemble and are waterproof.

Another suggestion would be to create overhead storage in your garage. Wooden planking can work as a platform where you can store boxes and other large items to keep them out of the way.

Conclusion

This is an opportunity to write down the answers to the questions posed earlier in this chapter. You may want to create a page each for your garage and one for the shed.

1. What are the major sources of frustration with your garage, and how could these be resolved?

_____

_____

_____

_____

_____

_____

2. Could you be using your garage, or shed, for other useful purposes e.g. create space for other activities?

_____

_____

_____

_____

_____

_____

3. Make a note of the new systems you're going to put in place to handle the multiple services of the garage (or shed).

_____

_____

_____

_____

_____

_____

CHAPTER NINE

DOWNSIZING TO A SMALLER ABODE

Downsizing is one of those words few people had heard of a decade ago. While moving from a house to somewhere smaller isn't new, more and more of us are considering this option and many are taking the plunge. Moving from one abode to a new one is often life changing, and whether the move is prompted by a sad or difficult circumstance or not, it can be looked at as a fresh start and an opportunity to create a completely new living environment.

There are numerous reasons why people move from a large house or villa to somewhere smaller. These people roughly fall into two camps: those who do so as a lifestyle choice and those doing so through some sort of external pressure. The decluttering practicalities are similar for both groups, but before getting to that it is worth spending time thinking through some of the circumstances and issues involved as once started, downsizing can be something that can be difficult to reverse. Trading in your house for a flat, or two flats if a couple are separating, is a huge decision and oftentimes once you've downsized to a smaller property, it can become a semi-permanent arrangement.

Here are some potential reasons for downsizing.

Existing property is too large

Large properties need more loving care and energy than smaller ones and can become a millstone. Even if there is only a couple living in a five bedroom detached home, there's heaps of housework, perhaps a large lawn to cut and garden to tend, a list of maintenance jobs as long as your arm, including re-decorating inside and out, unblocking gutters, trimming hedges and so on. The place may have been ideal when filled with a family, but once the children have moved on and have homes of their own the property will have probably outlived the purpose it was bought for i.e. as a family home.

The beauty of downsizing in this instance, particularly if you've opted for a flat, is that once a flat has been decluttered it can be cleaned up in next to no time. A blessing if you only get fifteen minutes notice before the arrival of guests. Knowing this makes flat dwelling seem attractive to owners of large homes who are burdened with a list of domestic chores, and having a cleaner and gardener to do these chores doesn't necessarily mean all of these jobs get done. While an average flat can be re-decorated over a couple of weekends, there is always something that needs to be done to a large house and by the time you get to the end of a very long job list it's time to start all over again. And if you are renting rather than buying, a leaky tap, broken window, or a need to repaint the property becomes your landlord's problem not yours.

Even if you are downsizing from a five-bedroom house to a two bedroom bungalow, you may opt for a property with a small outdoor area or at least low maintenance garden and lawns. This type of low maintenance scenario is appealing as one gets older and no longer has the energy or inclination to tackle heavier work often required for outdoor areas. Or it may be that those with busy lifestyles make choices which allow for more time to enjoy a social life rather than working on the house.

Existing property is too expensive

Generally the larger a property the more it costs. Apart from paying more in rent or mortgage repayments, you can expect to pay higher rates, have larger heating and lighting bills and pay extra for the upkeep of the property.

It is also a sad fact that some people have to re-locate somewhere smaller as they become a victim of redundancy. Others may have had to take a job that pays much less than they were getting and find they can no longer afford a large property. Deciding to downsize to an apartment, or a much smaller home, is therefore a less expensive option.

Divorce or separation

An additional disagreeable bi-product of marital breakdown is that one or both parties may have to move to smaller premises. Sometimes a husband moves out into a bedsit leaving his wife and children with the house, or the family home has to be sold to fund separate accommodation.

Widowhood

The loss of a partner may change the use of a house and a widow or widower may feel that she or he no longer requires as much space, or has a diminished appetite for running a large home. After Peter's father died his mother gave the family home to one of his brothers in return for being given a newly created granny flat. This freed her from housework and gardening chores and encouraged her to travel more, as well as relieving Peter's brother from finding monthly mortgage repayments.

It's often also comforting to relocate to a smaller home when losing a life partner, as one is less likely to feel that they are 'rattling around' in a flat as they would in a large house. If moving to a block of flats, a widow/widower is also more able to make new friends with neighbors, as well as benefiting from having people nearby.

Getting older/reduced mobility

Another big advantage of a flat over a traditional house is that most are on the same level so that climbing stairs is something you only do in other people's homes. Getting up and down stairs really becomes a problem when someone can only get around with the aid of a walker or a wheelchair.

Again, in a block of flats there will be neighbors who can help in a case of need, and also provide company if one is feeling lonely.

Funding a new life

Trading in a family home for something smaller is likely to provide a surplus. This money could be used in any number of creative ways. In the USA there are a surprisingly high number of elderly people who no longer have a fixed address but travel the continent in large campervans. Email, Skype, and mobile telephones ensure these nomadic converts stay in contact with family and friends. After decades of being tied to a particular location due to employment or their children's education it can be wonderfully freeing not to stay put in one place.

Time and energy invested in a house could be re-directed so that former owners could use funds to cruise the world, going to concerts, indulge in expensive hobbies like following a sports team around or any number of things that would once have seemed impossible.

One of Angella's friends did this a number of years ago—her dream was to travel New Zealand under her own steam, so she sold her Auckland property and bought a beautifully fitted out mobile home. She loved the lifestyle, discovering new places and meeting new people, and was often known to park her mobile home near a beach so she could watch the glorious sunsets and sunrises from the comfort of her mobile home. She had many an amusing anecdote to relate as she travelled New Zealand's sometimes narrow country roads, and laughed as she recounted often being stopped by livestock peacefully ambling down the middle of the road.

Funding a new life #2

Others trade in a family home in a suburb or rural location so they can move into a vibrant city centre where property is smaller but costs more. City dwelling is different from living out of town in a number of ways, firstly there is likely to be better public transport so you can get around a city without a car. Shops, art galleries, museums, sporting venues, concert halls, cinemas and a range of places to eat are often within easy reach. For many this can be a more attractive lifestyle, more suited to changing circumstances and worth trading in from a larger property.

The big cull

For whatever reasons you have decided to move into a smaller abode, the next set of decisions are going to be similar whether it is a free choice or one that has been imposed on you.

Angella has a flair for finding space in people's houses by re-ordering and re-arranging possessions so everything seems more ordered and spacious. Normally things that get thrown out or given away have long since had any use or value to the current owners.

But even Angella, or other top decluttering professionals, cannot pour the contents of a large property into one that is much smaller. She can't, if you like pour a gallon of household chattels into a sherry glass. It just can't be done.

However if you follow this process you should be able to reduce the flabby excess baggage that accumulates when you have lots of space, as well as the extra things no longer needed in a smaller dwelling.

Ideally it helps if you have answers to the following questions:

- What am I (we) moving to?
- Will my new location change the way I (we) live?
- How is my (our) life going to change?
- What do I (we) need and can't do without in a new home?
- Is this a temporary or permanent arrangement?

The circumstances in which you move may make it difficult to answer some of these questions but the more you know the better you will be able to make informed decisions. Let's look at each in turn.

What am I (we) moving to?

You are moving from a large villa to a tiny flat, or maybe a bach. Apart from having one instead of four bedrooms, your new kitchen may be a tiny corridor that estate agents call a galley, a shower room with a toilet rather than a family bathroom, an en-suite off the master bedroom and another toilet by the living area, no garage, no garden shed let alone a garden, and no dining room or study. Currently your walk in wardrobe is pretty full and the new flat has a small free standing job that would take about a fifth of your collective clobber. You get the picture.

Once you're clear on how much space you will have in your new home, you will have a better idea of what you need. Assess what is no longer necessary, for example furniture—if you are moving to a smaller house, and don't see yourself moving at any time in the future back into a large property, then there's no point in putting extra furniture into a storage unit.

By selling what you don't need on Trade Me or EBay, you can earn yourself some extra cash to maybe buy furniture more suitable for smaller premises. Garage sales are also a great way of getting rid of excess belongings and turning it into cash. And there are numerous charities who will take anything from furniture, to clothes, and books.

Will my new location change the way I live?

You're moving from next to the sea to an inner city dwelling. Currently space is no object and the concrete patch you park your vehicles on is a small car park where the boat you use for fishing expeditions and the kayak rest between infrequent outings. The city flat comes with an option to rent enough space to park a tiny hatchback in an underground car park and that's it. But you are some distance from anywhere you can use your 'toys' and the novelty and pleasure of using them has long worn off.

This is the time to look carefully at items you will no longer use, such as the boat and kayaks. If you're going to move to an inner city apartment, you may not even require a second car as you'll no doubt be walking to your destinations much more often.

How is my (our) life going to change?

Circumstances that made you decide to move are likely to provide clues. Lifestyle changes often occur when we move to a new home, whether we have moved to another city or perhaps from city life to rural life.

If you've moved from the city to the country, and have decided you are going to have a more laid back lifestyle, you'll probably no longer have use for all those business suits, briefcase, or boxed files of work papers.

Conversely if you are moving from a suburban home to a city apartment, you might completely redo your furnishings to be more in keeping with a chic city loft. You'll be closer to cultural and social activities so your wardrobe may also go through some changes.

What do I need and can't do without in my new home?

The short answer to this question is that most of us need a lot less stuff than we actually own. No one for example needs a foot spa whatever the advertisers tell you. Indeed just about anything advertised on telly is not really needed by anyone, that's why advertisers try and brainwash us into buying amazing exercise equipment which will make us toned and taut, or muscled.

Angella almost blushes as she mentions the fancy exercise thingy which promised lovely firm stomach muscles, and which has been under her bed since she bought it. Definitely one of those misguided moments.

Is this a temporary or permanent arrangement?

Your answer to this question will determine whether you keep many of your belongings and furniture, or not. If you're moving to smaller premises for a short period, for example while you are waiting for your lovely new big house to be built, then you will probably want to temporarily use a storage unit for the larger bulkier items which will definitely not fit into your temporary home. If you are doing this remember to label any boxes you put in the storage unit so it's clear what each contains.

If it is going to be a permanent move to a smaller house or apartment, then either sell or give away (or both) absolutely anything that you're not going to want or need in the future. There is no point in incurring the costs of a storage unit to store furniture and boxes of belongings that you will never use again.

This is the time now to make your assessment.

Assessment

With notepad and pen in hand, go from room to room and write your lists:

- What to keep: can't live without it / definitely need
- What to sell (or even leave for the next occupant of the house)
- What to give away
- What to store (if applicable)

You will probably want to consult with anyone else who is moving into the new home with you: spouse, kids etc, as they will no doubt have firm ideas on what they wish to keep. They might like to make their own list, with the caveat that some culling is required.

Keep in the front of your mind what your new place looks like and how much space is available. You could also take a photo of each of the rooms in your new home and have those displayed in front of you as you do your assessment of your belongings.

163

As you go through the house, don't forget to open all the cupboards and drawers, and check the nooks and crannies. And of course you'll need to also make an inventory of the garage, shed and attic.

Before you go through the list of items below for your decision making process, please bear in mind that we can become prisoners of our possessions. There is a certain sweet pleasure in living a more minimalist lifestyle, and there is often a tremendous feeling of freedom when we let go.

Books

Angella and Peter are both avid readers and love their books. However, even they have found that there can come a time when the multitude of books actually starts to take over the home. It is worthwhile taking the time to really assess those that you will read again, those you will definitely want to hold onto such as classics and good non-fictions. And then among all of these will probably be a bunch of novels you've read once and won't read again, and possibly some very old self-help books that have been superseded by updated versions—these are the ones you can give to a second-hand bookshop. Kids books which they have grown out of can find a happy home at a children's hospital.

Many of us keep certain books for sentimental reasons, especially our early childhood books, however if there's absolutely no room for them in your new home, then perhaps you could pass them on to your children, grandchildren, or even your neighbor's children. It's a delight to see someone else enjoying a book that you loved as a child.

Clothes

How many clothes do we need anyway? Pundits have it that we only wear 20% of our wardrobe 80% of the time. So what happens to the rest of the gear?

Well, we've probably been holding on to it because "I'll fit into it again one day", or "that was an expensive piece and I can't throw it away", or "you never know when I'm going to need that fleecy lined windbreaker (even though I've only worn it once)".

You get the picture. Most of us can actually quite safely get rid of at least 50% of our clothes, and still find we've got plenty to wear.

This is a wonderful opportunity to really go through your wardrobe and decide what you love and wear often, and what you are probably never going to wear again.

Angella does this regularly and her local Hospice shop loves to see her walk through the door with bags of clothes.

If you're moving to a smaller home, the wardrobes will probably be small and rather than be tempted to 'store' your clothes that won't fit into the wardrobe, you might find it's more expedient to make the decision now as to what can go.

Music

Almost every household will have old music CDs etc which they haven't listened to in years. CDs may not be very big but dozens of them will still take up a lot of room. If you can fit them all into a cabinet or fancy storage box, then that's probably manageable, but if you do take the time to sift through and discard what you can, you'll then have space to buy more!

Kitchen equipment

We bet that as you do your inventory of your kitchen equipment, you'll find double ups and old fashioned appliances that have been long since replaced (but not thrown out). Now's the time to really pare down and create a super efficient kitchen which contains only items and appliances you actually use.

China, cutlery and glasses

These are items we also tend to hoard, for no earthly reason other than we don't tend to throw out china and glasses. If you're downsizing you won't need several dinner sets or more than one canteen of cutlery. In larger homes we tend to entertain on a grander scale, whereas in smaller apartments or the like there just isn't room to cater for eight or ten people.

If you have loads and loads of glasses, of all types, you might like to do a cull and give the very ordinary ones away to a charity shop. Why load up your cupboards with glasses and crockery that you aren't likely to use or need.

Pictures

If you are moving from a large house with loads of rooms and huge dining and living areas, you probably have dozens of pictures on the walls. For those of you making a permanent move to a smaller home, or flat, you will have to make some hard decisions on which are your favorites that you're going to take with you, and which you can give away or sell.

Small houses or apartments don't lend themselves to a lot of pictures on the walls as this tends to close the rooms in.

Linen and towels

If the kids have all left home and there are just two of you left, chances are you have stacks of linen. Again, we suggest you pare down to just a few sets of your favorite sheets and enough towels for both of you, and donate the rest.

Full size linen cupboards are notoriously lacking in apartments and smaller homes, and space for linen can often be allocated to just a few shelves inside the hot water cupboard.

Rather than trying to cram all your linen into such a small area you could use it for just the immediate linen needs, and keep the guest linen either in the guest room, if you have one, or store it in a container of a size that can slide under your bed or on top of your wardrobe.

Collections

These are often tricky, depending on the size of the items you've been collecting. Smaller items can work well in a glass display box which hangs on a wall.

Coin and stamp collections can sit neatly on book shelves, or in a wooden display box chosen specifically for small collectables.

Peter has a wonderful, very extensive, collection of old tobacco tins, which he has artistically displayed on a top shelf in his kitchen, and they add great color and interest to the kitchen.

Storage

We've talked about storage throughout this book so you will already have plenty of ideas. However, when downsizing, you will have even less space so if you are going to store items you will need to think creatively. There is now a huge variety of storage boxes available, many of which are attractive enough to stack unobtrusively in a corner of a room. These are great containers for all sorts of miscellaneous bits and pieces, photos, papers, magazines and such like.

Stuff you might consider throwing out (or giving away)

- The foot spa you've only used a few times after being given it for Christmas six years ago.
- Presents you've been given, that you always hated but felt you had to hold onto because they were 'gifts'.
- Absolutely any item that you've had tucked away/hidden because it wasn't your style at all, but you bought it in a mad moment and because it was expensive you felt you couldn't get rid of it. Give it to someone who'll love it.

Planning

Sit down with your various lists of what to keep, and what to sell or give away. This is the time to read through them again and make sure all of your belongings are on one of your lists.

You may wish to do this exercise as a family (if you are all moving together) so that you're encouraging each other to work through your lists. You can even make it a fun process—have a competition to see who can give away or sell the most items.

If you have taken photos of your new home to be, spread them out on a table and then look at your 'To keep' list and see if what you're keeping is going to work in the new place. This is an opportunity to decide if you really do need some items on your 'To keep' list. This may be a tough process so you might like to fortify yourself with a good glass of wine, or some fine coffee and a plate of scrumptious biscuits. Take it slowly and ideally without interruptions.

Implement

Do take this process one room at a time, this is much less stressful and you will have a clearer idea of what needs to be done if you're just tackling the job room by room. Have plenty of boxes on hand, and label them: what goes into storage, what can be given away, and rubbish bags for what you think can be thrown away.

This is a culling process and there will probably be a few things which aren't quite good enough to be given to charities, or other willing hands.

Your lists will guide you as to what needs to go into each box so the process should be fairly streamlined.

Evaluate

Your evaluation will take place when you've actually moved into your new smaller abode. As you unpack each room you'll quickly see whether you need to do another sorting/culling or whether you hopefully have planned just right and everything fits beautifully.

It may be that you have a few things which you really do want to keep, but which can be stored in containers stacked in the garage (if you have one), under beds, or on the top of wardrobes. There will always be items you need only occasionally, or seasonally, so these can be stored away in the meantime.

Questions & Answers

Q   For financial reasons we have to move from a large villa to
    somewhere much smaller. There is no way we could get all
    our old furniture into the new place as much of it is bulky
    and suited to larger rooms. The depressed market means that
    we would not get what these pieces are worth in the present
    climate and much of what we own has been in my family for
    generations so it would be good to be able to pass it on to the
    kids. Also we like to think that when things pick up we will
    be able to find a larger home again. What can we do?

A   Long term storage may or may not be an option in your particular
    case. Make an inventory of surplus items and shop around for
    storage facilities as prices do vary between different firms. You
    may find that you could save money by finding a storage company
    outside your city rather than in a central city location where the
    cost of living is high. There may even be better terms for long term
    storage. If nothing else this will give you a benchmark figure.

    It may also help to divide your surplus items into two groups,
    those that you want to keep at all costs and things that could be
    replaced at a later date. Culling by selling or giving away the latter
    group should make coping with everything else more manageable.
    Networking to see if you can find someone in your circle prepared
    to give your furniture an area of their house or garage space might
    seem a long shot but you never know. You may be lucky and won't
    know unless you try.

Case Study #1

Ewan Campbell describes moving out of a home he'd lived in for 17 years:

"I'll never forget the time I moved out of the marital home for what gossipy neighbors would call 'the other woman' during a time those same people might call my midlife crisis. No point in dredging up all that again. I moved out, period, and had no intention of moving back despite the pleas, nagging, tears, and emotional blackmail. I can be a heartless bastard sometimes. Anyway things went quiet then I got a phone call saying that if I didn't collect my clothes and other personal things they would be put in black bags and left outside.

I'd walked out of the family home and it didn't occur to me that half the contents were mine. I was feeling as guilty as hell and didn't want to make things even worse, and to be totally frank, I was only living in a small room and had nowhere to store anything, besides just having my car to transport what I could take.

In circumstances like these you take what is clearly only of use to you and more or less leave everything else. Apart from my clothes I took my books—we'd always had loads of books and they loosely fell into four categories: his, hers, ours and the kids'. 'His' books were ones I bought or had been given and were of no interest to anyone else. It was more or less the same with CDs but there were loads of old record albums that mostly were mine that sadly had to be left behind as I didn't have anything to play them on and didn't have the house space to store them either.

A few kitchen implements would have been handy, and had I thought about it I might have taken a potato peeler if we had a spare one and a saucepan or two, plus a few dinner plates but where do you stop? It wasn't long before 'other woman' and I would set up home in an unfurnished flat. OW was able to bring quite a few things to the party and I just had my clothes, books, music and DIY tools: I'd been the only person to ever use them except one time when my ex-wife tried to hammer a screw into the wall.

What would I have done differently today? Can't say, but I did learn a few things. Firstly how little you need to set up home and feel comfortable: a fridge, an oven or just a microwave at a push, a kettle and a few other odds and sods for the kitchen, some bedding and a mattress, basic seating and a radio. And that's it.

I improvised by making a bed base with a couple of forklift pallets, made a dining table from a cardboard box that had contained a chest freezer and did the old student thing of making shelving from planks and bricks. It was all rather romantic really. But even had things been different, I'm not sure I would have wanted much more from my former home. Things had been bought for that place and belonged there as a testimony to that time and relationship. I'd moved on and these things would have seemed out of place in a new setting and new relationship, while they still meant something for the people who'd been left behind.

All this happened a while back and I can't say I've missed any of the physical things I walked away from; it's only stuff after all and can always be replaced. People are something else."

Case Study #2

Lucy Simmons is 73. A year ago she moved out of the family home, where she had lived with her husband Jim who died two and a half years ago, to move into an apartment in a complex entirely full of other elderly residents.

"Moving here was the best thing that ever happened to me. Jim and I had lived in the same house in Church Road for 45 years. After we got married we stayed with my mum until we had enough money to put down a deposit. The house was in a bit of a state when we got it, but little by little we improved it as we could afford to. Jim did a lot of the work himself and it was our pride and joy. I suppose you'd say we were a traditional couple; he went out and earned the money while I mostly stayed at home and looked after our children and the home. He could make a cup of tea but that was about it, he worked hard and that's how it was. He'd been ill for a long time before he died and I nursed him at home almost to the end. When he died I got quite depressed, it took me the best part of a year to start to feel right again.

My boy Derek suggested that I ought to find somewhere smaller. "You ought to be taking it easier at your age" were his words. I've always liked to keep the place nice and tidy and go through the house with a vacuum cleaner most days along with other household chores. I'm not really one for change but he kept going on at me and eventually he told me about this place.

My daughter June wasn't as keen that I moved, I think that she and her husband had their eye on Church Road and wouldn't mind getting their hands on it after I'd gone but as my Derek said "never you mind what they say Mother, it's your welfare that matters now." When I saw this place I thought it was a bit small but it had everything I needed and once I put in my bits and pieces it seemed quite homely, and there were no stairs. I can climb stairs now but I was thinking of the future.

At first I didn't know what to do with myself then Doreen who lives next door invited me in for a coffee. She lost her husband five years ago and we have a lot in common so we soon became really good friends. I'm not sure when it started but one day she cooks the meat and I'll cook the vegetables and the next day it'll be the other way round and then we eat together. We generally go shopping together once or twice a week and we both go to the same club. This place doesn't take much looking after and I can't say I miss my old house cleaning chores. It seems a bit pointless when it's only me living there."

Conclusion

You might like to use these exercises as part of your planning process. Use an exercise book if you prefer.

1. What is the look I want to create in my next home: chic and minimalistic; homely and comfortable; traditional?

_____

_____

_____

_____

_____

_____

2. What are the positive thoughts I can have around this move, and how can I make the move easy and pleasurable?

_____

_____

_____

_____

_____

_____

3. What have I been holding on to forever, and why? Is it because Aunt
    Mabel gave it to me 20 years ago (but I never really liked it), or is
    it something I want to keep as memorabilia?

    _____

    _____

    _____

    _____

    _____

    _____

CHAPTER TEN

CREATIVE SOLUTIONS

This chapter is about finding creative ideas which will make all the difference in your home, and office. You've worked your way through this book and probably made plans, even if just in your head, for how you're going to declutter and reorganize each room. The ideas presented here include suggestions that don't necessarily fit into any of the other chapters and can be easily incorporated into your planning process. These suggestions range from making rooms look larger or cozier, to some innovative ideas for decorating with a purpose.

When working with clients, and also in her own home, Angella is always thinking about how she can create new ways to enhance and embellish a room so that it's performing at its best, and is a delight to the eye. We all want our homes to look attractive, while also being functional and comfortable to live in. Functionality and comfort do not need to be sacrificed in the name of beauty. We could go even further and claim that beautiful objects look great because they are functional, unfussy and easy to use.

Following are some of the ideas we've come up with which you could try.

How to make small rooms look larger

- We pretty much all know about not painting rooms in dark colors so the room is not diminished. However, there are those brave souls who paint a bedroom in a lovely deep rich color thereby creating a gorgeous cozy sanctuary.

- Keep every surface as clear as possible—nothing will make a room look cluttered, and smaller, more than over-burdened furniture surfaces.
- Something else to bear in mind with small rooms is to keep furniture to a minimum, for example instead of a large wooden bookcase which will take up floor space, use wall space with shelves or cubes for your books.
- A cleverly placed large mirror can create the illusion of a larger room. Or you could mirror an entire wall.
- Using glass as the main material for a dining table or coffee tables will enable a small room to seem more open, and larger, whereas large wooden tables will define space and make the room look smaller.

How to make large rooms look cozier

- Grouping seating, as in couches and arm chairs, into a defined area of a large room will create an inviting conversation area.
- If the room is a large open area dining room/lounge you can form divisions between the two areas either with strategic placement of furniture, or by placing some beautiful urns and large potted plants along an imaginary boundary line.
- A floor to ceiling shelving unit can become an area of interest and detract the eye from looking the length of a large room. The shelves can be a feature used to display a few favorite objects.

Hanging Pictures

It is said that lining pictures up along their top edges rather than the bottom of the frames creates a more polished presentation. However, individuality is a wonderful thing and the desire for a particular 'look' will definitely vary from person to person.

One clever idea we came across is to create paper templates of the artwork you want to hang, gently sticking the paper cut-outs on the wall in various different arrangements to help you to decide which will be the most pleasing.

Lighting

Here are a few points on lighting your home, some of which may be fairly obvious but still useful to note for those of us who may be more right brain than left brain oriented:

- Standing lamps could be replaced with wall mounted lights with a swing arm fixture, to save space and remove at least one item from an otherwise busy room.
- Use spotlights to light up a collection of favorite pieces and your artwork. Feature lighting can be in the form of track lighting, recessed lights, or strip lights.
- Gauge how much lighting to use for each room by how much natural light enters the room.
- Ideally you will want adequate reading light for any seating areas in a living room and lounge area.
- Light up wardrobes and storage closets with a door-activated ceiling light, or a pull-cord ceiling fixture. Do make sure though that the light fixture does not come into contact with any items in the wardrobe.

Clever Furniture with dual uses

Ottomans

Fabulous as foot stools and extra seating, ottomans often have storage capacity inside which can be used for magazines, books, and games. You can also use the surface of the ottoman as a coffee table simply by placing a large sturdy tray on top for your coffee/tea or glass of wine.

Coffee tables

Many coffee tables contain shelving underneath for magazines and books. If it is open type shelving, try to keep it as uncluttered as possible—cull magazines and just keep current books on show.

Coffee tables are unfortunately more often than not used as dumping grounds for all sorts of objects such as TV remotes, months old magazines and books you're no longer reading. Keep your coffee table pristine by keeping the surface clear of anything that is not absolutely essential, or decorative. You will see the difference if you follow this simple rule, and the room will look less cluttered too.

Chests

Traditional wooden chests are beautiful pieces, and are wonderful for storing all sorts of items such as linen, books and magazines, and favorite photo albums. They don't look out of place in a living area and can also be used as a coffee table.

Beds with Storage

If you're about to shop for a new bed, for you or the children, consider choosing something with built in storage compartments. Angella is still surprised to discover the majority of her clients have beds with absolutely no storage underneath because the mattress goes right to the floor. What a shame to lose out on such wonderful storage possibilities.

There is such a wide range of storage options with under bed drawers and even shelves. For example, drawers can take the place of a chest of drawers in a smaller bedroom, and also work well for storing out of season clothes, linen, and books. Drawers under a child's bed may contain their treasured toys and artwork.

Sofa beds

Sofa beds deserve a place in this section as they can provide an additional double bed as well as seating. In truth most are excellent as sofas and second rate as beds and a bit of a hassle to convert from one role to the other, plus you need to find somewhere to hide bedding during the day. On the other hand having a guest bed that is not too comfortable and placed in the lounge is as good a way as any for ensuring that visitors do not overstay their welcome. And innovative furniture design means handsome more user-friendly versions of sofa beds can be found.

Library chairs

Perhaps one of the best examples of a dual use piece of furniture is the so called library chair. In one guise it can be used as a seat, and can then effortlessly be turned into a stepladder. It performs both tasks equally well and saves space if you need it for both roles. And it's attractive enough so that you don't need to feel that you have to store it away or stack it in a corner.

Shelving

There is almost nowhere in the home that wouldn't benefit from an extra shelf or two and that includes bathrooms and laundries which definitely lend themselves to shelving for regularly used items. Kitchens hopefully have an abundance of shelves, and they can be handy in bedrooms for books and perhaps accessories.

The trick is to organize items on shelves so as not to create clutter. You can keep each shelf dedicated to specific items, or mix them a little as in the case of book shelves where you can use an ornament or two as book ends. When arranging items, keep in mind that shelves are open to view so it's important not to burden them with too many items.

Displaying Collections

On Shelves

A series of shelves along a wall or two lend themselves to beautifully displayed collections. A plain painted wall will also provide a wonderful backdrop to several shelves as home to a colorful collection of objects. And a clever little corner shelving niche can become a natty display of much loved photos.

In Cubes

A series of cubes atop each other can work well for collections of smaller objects, and cubes can also be attached to the wall at varying heights to create a sophisticated and charming display.

The 'anti-collection' Collection

Peter's Aunt Gunnel loves pigs. She lives in a small yet comfortable apartment in central Stockholm. Over the decades Gunnel has acquired every conceivable pig representation known to man. They are made of china, wax, resin, plastic, felt, knitted . . . and that is before you consider the pig posters, postcards, photos and drawings. Generally collections are displayed together as the sum of the total is greater than the individual parts.

What Gunnel has done is scatter her pig collection in each room in the apartment and moves them around from time to time. When her grandchildren and their friends visit many happy hours are spent locating as many examples as possible of these lovely creatures which pop up in unexpected places.

Novel Solutions

While most of us have little difficulty throwing out newspapers or magazines, we are more reluctant to part with our books. There may be the occasional cull where unwanted Jeffrey Archers get taken to a hospice shop to join other volumes by this same author, but unless we are downsizing most of our book collections grow year by year.

Books can be stored in a number of places, on shelves, in cupboards, and inside furniture such as ottomans. Some coffee tables include shelving which is an ideal spot for books you're reading now. Magazine boxes which can sit alongside the couch can contain current favorites.

If you're a book lover and have a multitude of much loved volumes, you may like to create a library area by dedicating a wall to shelving. If you don't have space in your main living areas, consider using a wall in the guest room.

Books of course come in different sizes and shapes and are consumed in vastly different ways. For the most part, novels and biographies are read in a few sittings and stored until someone else wants to read them, which is quite different from the way coffee table books are used. If you tidy up and relegate your expensive art books or ones containing lots of photos to inaccessible shelves the chances are that they will never be leafed through and enjoyed, therefore defeating the purpose of having them. It also follows that you are more likely to use a cookery book if it has a home in the kitchen.

Organizing Toys

Toy chests might seem a great invention. Once the little ones have been put to bed you can blitz the living room by throwing all kids' toys into the one place. However, if toys all get dumped into the same container, chances are that when searching for a particular toy your child may well have to upend the entire toy chest. We have visions here of a child immersed head first inside the toy chest while flinging toys out to the left and the right. This type of scenario could be avoided by using a number of storage containers or boxes, each designated by type, for instance Lego, soft toys, puzzles, DVDs and books.

When building their new home, Angella's sister-in-law, Debbie, designed a fabulous walk-in alcove off their living room. This long narrow room is her children's area and is completely dedicated to toys, DVDs and CDs, dressing up costumes, and books. Shelves are organized by specific item, and the dress up area even has little rails for hanging clothes.

You may also be able to put some shelving into a child's wardrobe space, or along a wall of the kid's bedrooms, so possessions can be sorted and popped into containers.

When children are small they don't usually need to use as much wardrobe space as we adults do, so inserting shelves into a wardrobe space allows special toys to be popped away, while still being at a level that a child can reach.

Organizing Shoes

We've talked about putting shoe organizers into the bottom of wardrobes in the Bedroom chapter. If you have a walk in wardrobe, there are numerous options for sorting women's shoes (yes, we probably do have a few more pairs than the average guy) . . . Shelves and drawers in a large wardrobe, preferably along the same wall, can be dedicated to specific type of shoes. If you pile too many shoes into cubby-holes, which are often a feature of walk in wardrobes, they not only become a jumbled mess, it's difficult to find what you're looking for quickly. And the shoes at the back get forgotten.

The rule of thumb is that you must be able to see your possessions—if they're hidden behind something else it's going to be a case of 'out of sight, out of mind'.

You can use shelves for shoe boxes, and if you take a photo of the shoe and tack it to the side of the box, it creates an easy to use system.

Certain shoes such as sports shoes, boots, and gardening shoes, can be better relegated to a corner of your garage in container units with large bin-like drawers. They don't take up much room, and each family member can have a designated drawer in the unit.

Accessories

Again, it's a female thing—we like to accessorize, and our challenge becomes how we can organize our many bags, scarves, and jewellery in such a way that they are all on view, and we can scoop up a piece on the run.

Of course guys have accessories too, but they're generally limited to belts and ties. Read on guys to the section on 'drawer organizers'.

A simple hat or coat stand creates a beautiful display of colorful handbags, which are all easily accessible and, also important, being hung they keep their shape. If you have the wardrobe space, then you can also get a hanging bag container which is quite clever.

Scarves can be draped over hooks (behind a wardrobe door for example), or on a coat stand, and a cork board is an ideal display system for necklaces, bracelets and even earrings. You use dressmaker's pins to hook the item onto the cork board.

Photos

Many of us will remember with a smile the days when we would sit for hours poring over ancient family photo albums, which inevitably took us on delightful trips down memory lane.

It now seems that with modern technology it's popular to keep photos on a disk, or simply stored on the computer, or on the internet.

For the purists among us who still boast dozens if not hundreds of actual photographs, there needs to be a system to keep them in good condition and which is also conducive to easy viewing.

Albums come in an endless variety of sizes and textures and are a work of art in themselves, well able to be left out on a coffee table to browse through at leisure.

Alternatively, a collection of attractive boxes enables your photos to be sorted and labeled by category i.e. friends and family, holidays, and even a box per family member. If you use visually appealing boxes you can create a display area for them on a shelf, or bookcase.

The photo wall

Lovingly getting round to putting all the old family photos into albums is something most people never quite get to do. It is not uncommon to discover a suitcase jam packed with packets of photos that also contain the negatives. This is a pity as these snapshots are often gems and record happy times, changing fashion and dreadful haircuts.

One creative solution is to make a montage of photos covering a bathroom wall or any other area that is not affected by direct sunlight. You will need to laminate this collection or at least cover them with perspex to prevent damage, however a little effort in putting a collage such as this together could create a wonderful feature

You've been framed

There are many inexpensive picture frames that can be acquired in markets and inserting or changing a photograph only takes a minute or two. After a month or so we stop noticing a particular image so why not put together a cluster of frames on a wall then rotate photos every few weeks to keep the collection fresh and interesting.

Organizing Miscellaneous Items

Travel items

Those of us who are regular travelers will usually have collected assorted items directly related to travel such as international plugs, socks and a pillow for the plane, jetlag tablets, mini containers of cosmetic creams, and drawstring bags for shoes. Add to that collection such essential items as passports and any other travel documents, as well as travel guides, maps and brochures you are likely to use again and you discover that you have quite a lot of travel miscellany.

The last thing you want to have to do when you're packing for a trip is to have to search for these items, and usually one or two will be forgotten entirely. Gather together everything related to travelling and put it all into a box, or perhaps into an overnight bag which can tuck into a corner of a wardrobe or under the bed. We promise you'll be delighted when it comes time to pack for your next trip.

Drawer organizers

There are all kinds of imaginative systems now to organize items in drawers. Drawer dividers, some of which are made of artfully constructed cardboard shapes, keep items orderly and easy to find. Also rolling items, such as ties, prevents them from becoming creased. It comes back to what you can see you will use, which applies to drawers and wardrobes. By storing our garments, and 'pretties', neatly we are also prolonging their life.

Desk Organizers

Again, it's a matter of gathering together like items so they're accessible and tidy. Office desks often fall prey to extreme clutter with loads of small fiddly items such as business cards, stapler, scissors, pens etc etc.

A neat container for your pens, alongside another which holds other small miscellaneous items, quickly organizes your desk. You can even find all sorts of containers in your home which will do the job e.g. a mug can be used for pencils and pens, and a box can store scissors, stapler and post it notes.

Bric-a-brac

Over time most of us acquire a collection of objects of little practical use that we are reluctant to throw away. These items may be gifts we've had for decades, and kept because they are pleasing to the eye. Ornaments and trinkets deserve to be seen yet can easily clutter a room or take over a worktop. Imposing some rules on a motley assortment of objects can make the whole greater than the sum of its parts. For example if you cluster a group of random objects, that by themselves may look like junk, by color or material you could create an interesting corner of a room.

Peter was given one of his grandfather's top hats and the original leather case. By adding this container to some ancient leather suitcases his bedroom has a pleasing focal point and the suitcases are a useful place to archive old documents.

Sometimes people throw together sea shells, a few pieces of drift wood and a painting of a bathing hut to brighten up a dull bathroom alcove.

Bookcases are not just for books

Books and book shelves are a wonderful backdrop for all sorts of other objects: pictures, plants, china dolls, candles, model cars, postcards; the list is endless. Apart from providing somewhere to display things that don't seem to belong anywhere in particular, these objects can add a dash of color and wit to what might otherwise be a po-faced part of the house. CD players and speakers can also be hidden among your book collection, placing it here not only frees up another part of the room but could be positioned near to your CD collection.

Stairwells

Apart from getting occupants from one storey to the next, stairways are often the most undervalued and not thought about parts of a home. In some houses you might find a few bland pictures and that's it. Stairways can instead be converted into areas of interest. One home we saw exhibited the owner's collection of fishing rods above the banisters.

Using this area to display objects not only frees up other parts of the house but is a great way to ensure that visitors get to see things you are justly proud of. And a collection of paintings and art objects can look wonderful displayed up the stairway.

And last but not least: some more practical organizing ideas

The home diary

Many of us keep a personal paper or electronic diary. We may use it to keep dental or hairdresser appointments and other commitments, as well as social activities. Families or house sharers, it seems to us, could easily emulate ward diaries used by nurses. Sometimes these are called a 'communication book' and they serve as a reminder for tasks as well as appointments.

A simple spiral bound diary with a day per page can be used to inform someone to take out the wheelie bin, buy milk, hang around to let in an electrician who is coming to fix the washing machine, or phone the plumber. Some households use a whiteboard or leave messages attached with a magnet to the fridge. Apart from being messy, messages can be lost and there is no way to demonstrate that one particular person is buying the milk or has returned the library books. A simple tool like this not only ensures that mundane tasks do not get forgotten but also helps foster responsibility by everyone sharing a home.

Remembering website logons and passwords

The 'Favorites' or 'Bookmarks' sections on the Internet are great for storing favorite website links. A simple and quick way to organize your website favorites is to create specific folders within the Favorites/Bookmarks menu, this saves you having to scan down a long list of links. Categories of folders could include network organizations, business websites, travel sites, inspirational, and personal.

However, as most of us become members of a large number of websites, we still need to record somewhere the Logon and Password for each site. Angella has a simple system which works for her. She uses a small hardcover notebook (pocket size is fine) with one section of the notebook containing a list of websites that are recommended, or that she plans to visit. At the back of the book she has her list of websites that she's a member of, together with the username and password clues for each website.

The notebook should be kept somewhere safe as this is not information that you want to be readily accessible to just anyone. And where she wants to retain a password as confidential she creates a code word or writes the password in another language. They need to be good 'memory jolts' so the password immediately comes to mind (but wouldn't make sense to anyone else).

Library notebook

If you are an avid reader like Angella, who takes six or seven books out of the Library at a time, you may want to keep a record of what you've read so you don't end up getting a book out more than once. The same will apply whether you are a regular attendee at your local Library, or if you have a favorite bookshop where you buy your books.

Again, we suggest a pocketsize notebook, and you may find it useful to get one which is alphabetized, such as an address book. As with any type of filing system, you can choose whether to list your books by author, or perhaps by category. Angella lists by the author's surname, and each time she gets a new set of books from the Library she makes sure she writes down the book title under the author's name in her notebook.

The advantages of this type of system are twofold: you don't make the mistake of getting the same book twice, and you can take the notebook with you as a reminder of your favorite authors and go straight to that section of the library or bookshop.

You can use the same sort of notebook as shown above for the website logons and passwords, as the dividers will allow you to keep your various lists separate and organized by section.

Questions & Answers

Q During recent years I have started to collect egg cups. I now have more than I can cope with yet family and friends can't go to a garage sale without coming back with even more of these objects. They are spreading like mushrooms onto every surface in the kitchen making the place feel cluttered. It seems churlish to ask everyone to stop buying them but what else can I do?

A Egg cups seems to us a great idea for a collection. They come in all sorts of sizes, colors, shapes and materials and they are often wonderful examples of witty, off the wall designs. It wasn't quite an egg cup, but we have seen an egg container consisting of a dozen monks, and when filled with eggs each monk had a bald pate.

   People often start accumulating a collection without realizing how easily numbers can grow. One solution might be to find an unexciting area of the house, like a hall or corridor, and build customized shelving. Floor to ceiling shelving could accommodate thousands of egg cups which would not only add interest to that part of the house but also provide a talking point and must visit place for future visitors.

Q My partner is a film buff. His knowledge about Charlie Chaplin, Harold Lloyd, Buster Keaton, and the Marx Brothers is truly remarkable. He also has a huge collection of DVDs, reference books and much else related to his passion. We have a home cinema set up in our lounge which is fine as the speakers are concealed and you hardly notice the screen when it's rolled up. It would be logical to put up shelving in the lounge to house his films but if we did that it would clash with the Oriental furniture and art we acquired overseas. What do you suggest?

A While it makes sense to organize your kitchen so that for instance saucepans are near the hob it is less important that DVDs are next to a DVD player. Each film takes at least 90 minutes to watch and it is unlikely that you are going to watch more than a couple during one sitting.

Why not have a dedicated storage area, which could for example be a glass cabinet, to display your partner's collection in another part of the house, perhaps including film posters, monochrome photographs of the silver screen stars and Hollywood ephemera.

Q **My wife fell down the stairs and broke her hip. She will be coming out of hospital soon but will not be able to climb stairs for some time to come. Our bedroom and the only toilet are on the first floor. We have a small room on the ground floor that we could use as a temporary bedroom for her but it is not big enough to take a single bed let along somewhere to put her clothes. What do you suggest?**

A   Have you thought about getting one of those Z beds? Models vary, some of the older ones have rather flimsy mattresses but there are others which have thicker mattresses which are a lot more comfortable.

The Z bed folds out front-wise from a comfy chair to become a bed. This could be set up in the small downstairs bedroom without taking up too much room, and therefore leave room for your wife's clothes. If the room doesn't have a wardrobe then you could get a standing rail that she can hang her clothes on; and some boxes or a suitcase to store the rest of what she needs.

A commode would save her trying to get upstairs during the night to the toilet. You could check out a nearby nursing home and see if you can borrow one for a few months until your wife is able to climb stairs again.

Conclusion

You might like to use these exercises as part of your planning process. Use this space or an exercise book if you prefer.

1. What items in your home desperately need to be organized? List them here along with possible solutions in this chapter.

    _____

    _____

    _____

    _____

    _____

    _____

2. Think about furniture or other items in your home that can have a dual use and therefore act as space savers.

    _____

    _____

    _____

    _____

    _____

    _____

3. What creative solutions in this chapter could work in your home and/or office.

_____

_____

_____

_____

_____

_____

Chapter Eleven

Life after Clutter

If you have been systematically working through this book and sorting out your home a room at a time, it will have been transformed. A nagging doubt may remain: your home may have been decluttered but will it stay that way?

One of the surprising by-products of decluttering your home is how quickly you forget how things used to be. In the same way that you forget how your lounge looked before it was redecorated, you soon can't remember where things used to be and there's no longer those crazy hunts to find a light bulb, a measuring jug or a pair of socks.

We recommend that you go round and take photographs of each room before you start to declutter. Open up drawers and make a visual record of what is there now. It won't take long and these images will be oddly comforting to look back on down the line when the new systems have been bedded down. Who knows, this collection of before pictures, paired up with after shots of how it looked following your declutter could be the basis of a book to rival this one.

At the same time it is a good idea to make a written record of what your cluttered house or flat was like to live in. In particular note your emotions, specific stressful incidents and how anxious or depressed you felt. This is a perverse pleasure that can be enjoyed when these symptoms become a thing of the past. And of course by looking back at how it was and how it felt, you will be much less likely to want to go there again at any time in the future.

How you know your home is now a decluttered space . . .

The property

You know when you are in a clutter-free home. It's more than just tidy; there is a sense of order and calm. If you cook in someone else's organized and uncluttered kitchen for the first time you will find it surprisingly easy to find things whether its tea bags, garlic cloves or a saucepan. Open a cupboard or drawer and you will know immediately that it's the right spot for the item you are looking for.

Many people assume that decluttering a home requires throwing everything away and just having a barren, minimalist look that was briefly in vogue back in the eighties. This is not true. To live the sort of varied lifestyles most of us seem to these days requires possessions, whether it is clothing for different occasions, sports equipment needed for this activity or apparatus to help us make meals. Homes have more than a purely functional purpose, as stated elsewhere in this book, so it would be perverse to remove those quirky items that celebrate what makes each family or occupant unique. Decluttered homes seem to strike the right balance between the twin functions of being a well oiled machine and a buttress to protect its occupants from the rest of the world.

We are all affected by the environment we live in. Restricting the amount of space each of us has is likely to make us increasingly fretful and agitated and it also reduces our ability to be creative. Organizing and decluttering a room might not make a room bigger but it can certainly make it feel more spacious and therefore a much more relaxing area to be in.

Taking each room in turn once your home is decluttered you'll soon notice many positive effects such as some of these we've described below.

The kitchen

Cooking and making meals will be more enjoyable. You won't have to hunt for ingredients in any one of three drawers, equipment will be stored near where it's used and an inviting kitchen may encourage others to cook so what once might have been a chore performed by a single person could be a shared pleasure.

You'll probably also find you're more inclined to entertain at home, and invite friends into the kitchen for a shared glass of wine and a chat while you're cooking dinner. And you can enjoy your kitchen as a hub of the home and an inviting area where family congregate at the end of the day.

And of course, decluttered kitchens are not only easier to keep tidy as everything has a home, but are also easier to keep clean and hygienic.

The living areas

Lounges or living areas will feel more relaxing and inviting, again there will be a place for everything. You'll find it easy to wind down of an evening and enjoy the sense of peace that is achievable when areas are clutter free. Specific books, CDs, DVDs, and magazines are ordered in a way that makes them easy to locate.

And there is unlikely to be a panic when guests arrive as these rooms remain in a state that causes owners to feel pride rather than humiliation when outsiders enter.

Bedrooms

Decluttered bedrooms feel soothing. Beds and comfy chairs in bedrooms will no longer be dumping grounds, and surfaces will be clear so you'll feel that sense of calm as soon as you enter the room. You'll probably even find that you sleep better without all those distracting objects around you. There's something about a calm environment to induce a peaceful night's sleep.

The kids' rooms are no longer hazard areas with tiny pieces of toys scattered around the bedroom ready to gouge unsuspecting little feet, and toys are actually being kept in their respective containers.

In particular, wardrobes will have been culled of clothing that is no longer worn, and what remains is sorted by type and color. For instance trousers will be hanging together, and likewise with suits, dresses, shirts and skirts. And sorting them by color makes it easier to see what is available. Arranging clothing in this way makes selecting what you want to wear, and mixing and matching, remarkably easy. The old cry, 'I've nothing to wear' was often due to not being able to see the wood from the trees.

The home office

A clear desk and an uncomplicated filing system will go a long way to ensuring your home office functions like clockwork. The unpaid bill or invoice can be found and processed and a clear desk means that you can get onto your computer and start working straight away. You've discovered what a pleasure it is to work in this type of uncluttered environment.

The garage or workshop

Small jobs around the home like putting up a picture can be done in no time when you know where to find a hammer, hook, stepladder, spirit level and measuring tape.

Big jobs seem less intimidating when your tools are organized and you can get to the workbench with ease. In fact you'll probably find yourself volunteering for a few more DIY jobs around the house . . .

It's also an added advantage when you can eke out a working space in the garage for your gardening supplies.

Staying decluttered

Day to day

It would be lovely to imagine that decluttering a home is the end of the process; that once the kitchen, living room, study and the rest have been sorted you can all live happily ever after without ever having to worry about the intrusion of clutter again. If only. The organizational structures put in place will only work if they are practical, understood by all members of the household, and used.

A decluttered area is likely to be tested soon after it has been sorted. Someone scoops up the post, the local newspaper and junk mail and takes it to the kitchen and deposits it on the virgin worktop. A gauntlet has been thrown down: do you leave it there and start a new paper mountain or make immediate decisions about where each item goes? A similar challenge occurs when you walk in the house and remove your coat. Do you hang it up in the cloakroom or throw it on a dining room chair for now? After all it's getting late and you'll need the coat in the morning.

If you have been used to leaving clothes scattered around the house the additional effort of putting something away may seem a hassle. Give in to the urge to drape the coat over the back of the chair and you will be back to square one in no time; hang it up and you will not only be reinforcing the new structure but also leading by example to other people who live with you.

Setting up new habits

What is required is a changed mindset. When Angella is working with a client she's not just looking at their physical environment. She is delving into what's beneath the current habits around the clutter, and checking any hoarding tendencies.

As we've mentioned in the first chapter of this book, there are reasons why we allow our living and working environment to become un-user friendly, however these reasons are no longer serving us. So, yes, there does need to be a shift of mindset and new habits created that will ultimately bring relief. It's really about finding the motivation, and self interest, to set up a system and decide to stick to it.

Why don't you have a family meeting and get everyone's commitment to the declutter project. And to using storage or disposal systems you set up for each room once it's been decluttered from that moment onwards.

If these systems are practical this is not as difficult or as time consuming as it might at first seem. It is also surprising how quickly you can create new habits and if the systems and structures you've put in place during your declutter project are explained to everyone so they make sense, then it's more likely that the rest of the family will use them.

Ideally once an item has been used it's returned by the 'user' to its correct home. Alternatively, your family might prefer to commit to tidying the house at the end of each day by removing junk from worktops, and putting equipment back in its home so that everyone wakes up next morning to a clutter free home. You might even want to try both systems then vote on which one seems to work best. The main goal is to get buy-in on either returning everything to its home immediately after it's been used, or doing it at the end of the day.

The thing is, with practice we all get better about making fast decisions, deciding what is junk and ought to go straight into the recycling bin and what is useful information that needs to be retained.

The trick is walking the junk over to the bin at the time, and having either a file box or appropriate folders or containers nearby so that useful information to be retained can be tucked away. Smart use of a labeling machine and having spare files and/or storage boxes on hand helps. This means when something 'new' comes into the house a box or filing system can be set up for it immediately, if one doesn't already exist. Labeling machines come into their own when it comes to creating storage systems as stacking boxes or bins works best when each is clearly labeled.

Allocation of chores

Angella also asks questions about how the family works together as a unit, who does what—and is there an allocation of chores or does one person end up doing the lion's share. She finds if it's just one person who's usually doing most of the chores then a sense of helplessness can build up if it's felt that other members of the family aren't contributing their share. If it's Mum who's doing all the putting away of the family's gear, all the time, then she might want to look at changing this set up.

During the family meeting, you can use that time to get agreement on a shared jobs schedule. Why not let everyone in the family enjoy that sense of satisfaction felt when a job has been well done, and this can include clearing up and creating a nice tidy living environment.

If you're decluttering the entire home, then everyone in the family will be benefiting from the project. So it stands to reason that they're all going to need to look at how they can help keep it maintained.

You can also look at how you can make this fun, for example, with kids you can make a game of clearing up toys and putting them in their containers. You can even give a prize to the child who has the most uncluttered room at the end of the week.

Shopping—no more overbuying

It's a fact that almost everyone has fallen into this trap. What do you do when you can't find something—go out and buy it! It's highly possible that you already have at least three of these items scattered throughout the house, but they remain elusive when you most need them.

Of course, once the house has been decluttered this won't happen anymore. At that point you can set up your shopping system. We suggest a simple whiteboard, or blackboard, be used as an ongoing shopping list by all the family. As an item is getting close to being used up put it on the list. A useful rule of thumb is to put an item on the list as soon as you've started using the last one e.g. batteries, light bulbs, printer consumables.

Shopping and Replacing

What do we mean by this? Well, we will always shop—it's such a pleasurable activity and something most of us love to do. However, what happens when we bring home our lovely new purchases? We end up with more stuff! So the solution here is quite simple, as you bring new things into the home, you pass on or discard what you no longer need or want. This is the only way you'll remain uncluttered.

Angella adores shopping and some of her favorite buys are shoes, clothes, jewellery and books (not necessarily in that order). She has long since come to the realization that one can actually have too many pairs of shoes, items of clothing and jewellery. And any books she wants to read she gets out of the library. So Angella regularly culls out her wardrobe and accessories, and passes these things on to friends and family, or charities. By doing this she is actually creating space to allow her to shop again!

A helpful thought process when shopping is, for example, if you're looking at buying a new pair of shoes—are they replacing a pair at home that you no longer wear, or that are worn out? If you're not replacing shoes, then think to yourself—do I have room to store this extra pair of shoes? In other words, you are continually keeping in mind your storage capacity, and deciding on the spot if you really do need that item, or not.

Mini decluttering sessions

Angella practices what she preaches. She lives in an uncluttered home but it is only able to remain that way through periodic mini decluttering sessions. It's not that the systems break down and coffee cups migrate to a cupboard reserved for plates, but rather homes and the people who live in them are dynamic entities that grow and change. New things find their way in and our needs change.

The good news is that a mini decluttering session is not nearly as time consuming as the original one was.

There are usually certain areas in a home which will be more inclined to gather clutter than others. For example, Angella finds her office cupboards, linen and wardrobe storage areas are the places she needs to declutter more regularly than others.

Office areas in particular most often need a mini declutter session as this is where we are busier and are inclined to want to focus on work tasks rather than keeping files, papers and research material organized in their storage areas. The important thing to remember here is that once you have created your storage and filing systems, then a mini clear up is just that—a regularly scheduled pulling together of all the papers and then putting them in their allocated systems, and deciding what you no longer need to keep.

You'll know when it's time to conduct a mini declutter—it's usually when you can feel that frustration start to creep in again.

On average, office cupboards will probably need to be organized back into their systems every four to six months, and other storage areas as needed.

Wardrobes can benefit from a mini declutter at the change of season, when you store away last season's clothes, and assess what you've got for the new season.

Pantries and fridges need to be decluttered more often so you don't risk dragging out expired foods for dinner.

Involving others

Getting in an expert

As hopefully we have demonstrated in earlier chapters, the principles of decluttering are fairly straightforward: you start with an assessment of a particular room or area, make a plan, work through it and modify it in the light of how it works in practice.

Sometimes however it is difficult to see the wood from the trees and if a home is super cluttered and chaotic then the effort, and wherewithal, required to transform this into somewhere desirable just feels too daunting.

In these cases the solution may be to get in an expert.

A decluttering expert offers a number of different services. In essence they consist of:

- A fresh pair of eyes
- Expertise in decluttering
- Ideas on how to best use available space
- Knowledge of storage systems
- An ability to chunk up jobs and get each part done efficiently
- An ability to share and teach these skills
- And there is certainly an element of coaching to assist clients through the tough decisions

Employing an expert is a big commitment for yourself and your household. The mere act of picking up a telephone and booking an appointment is a way of demonstrating to yourself that you want to make changes to the way the home is organized. A fresh, expert pair of eyes is a great way to kick-start the process and make what might have seemed an impossible task seem straightforward.

Organized and tidy people are fundamentally no different from those who are disorganized. What is different is that they are shown, taught or have stumbled across techniques and systems that help them keep their house in order. This stuff can be taught and is a lot easier to learn than say driving a car or touch typing. And it can be learnt at any age. All that is required is an acceptance that your home is not working for you as well as it could, a desire to change and a willingness to try to do things differently.

Peter assumed that everyone used Angella in the way he and his ex did. Namely to sort out various areas in their home and the resulting solutions and tips given during these short sessions would make her redundant and she would go off and sprinkle her magic elsewhere.

There are certainly clients who use her in this way, and then there are others who tend to bring her back repeatedly as their circumstances change, such as when moving home, downsizing and so on. These clients are not necessarily interested in learning how to do this by themselves—they would rather have an expert come in and do the job for, and with them.

One of Angella's clients has in fact moved house five times, within the same city, but in completely different locations and different types of homes. This client called on Angella's services each time as every one of these houses had its own challenges and limitations. These challenges included fitting two separate home office/working spaces into a home which barely contained enough room for the entire family and all its belongings. It sometimes does take an expert eye to work out where everything will fit so that it works for everyone in the home.

Breaking the mold: becoming an ex-hoarder

Throughout this book we have stressed that we are not against possessions provided there is sufficient space to keep them. It might be helpful here to define what we mean by a 'hoarder' and 'hoarding behavior', and how it differs from a collector and collecting.

Hoarding

Hoarders hoard. There is almost something needy and pathological in the way some people acquire things for the sake of it. They have an urge to own and keep things regardless of the item's usefulness, value or aesthetic appeal. There is a reluctance to part with things even if they know objects serve no purpose now, or are ever likely to.

At its most extreme, hoarding behavior tends to repel others who may feel excluded and rightly recognize something is not quite right. Left unchecked, hoarding can become an obsession and symptoms can stifle and choke a room or even a whole house. There is generally no sense of order, just an accumulation of more and more clutter.

Collecting

While collectors collect they rarely seem possessed by their harmless collections. And while they may have built up a huge number of examples, there would seem to be a celebration going on and even people who may not share an interest in pottery teapots, thimbles or (dare we say it) tobacco tins, can be charmed by the variety and presentation of these objects. There is generally a sense of order and a collection is rarely allowed to take over and impede the way a home functions.

Collectors may be tempted to grow their collections but know when to stop, either because of insufficient space or funds. Hoarders don't.

While most of us have urges to hoard, most of us have enough insight to know when to stop, or have family or friends who we are able to listen to if we have become a little excessive.

In extreme cases medical intervention is required to treat the underlying cause of hoarding, but for the rest of us learning to give or throw away things we no longer need is freeing and can feel as therapeutic as shopping, and is a whole lot cheaper.

Case files

During the writing of this book Peter spoke to some of Angella's clients to get a sense of how decluttering had affected their lives. Their responses indicate ways this process can improve homes and families.

Gina, Auckland

"I've learnt to keep up with the decluttering as I go along. What I tended to do was to let things like papers pile up. I don't think I'm quite where I'd like to be. But I know a few things now. When I feel organized and when things are in place that helps the family and there's less stress. The more organized the parents are then the less stress there is in the home. Happy mother: happy home.

When you have kids you have to adapt and change. And one of the things that I've changed is now I aim to get things ready the night before, or I aim to get ready earlier because when there's children involved it takes time and it's too stressful to do it all in the morning. You always find that something's missing whereas if you knew the night before you could deal with it then.

Angella did a room by room assessment. The first time she came in and saw how everything was, our bedroom was untidy, there was no system in the kitchen for dealing with mail and all the notices that you get from school. She talked to us, had a look around, went away, wrote up an assessment for us and came back and said, "This is how I believe we can approach it."

Angella recalls: "This two page assessment became our work plan for every room in the house. It included in several cases moving furniture from one room to another (where it could be put to better use), creating an uncluttered working area for Gina in a corner of their lounge room, and a detailed plan for every room putting in place systems and structures which worked for everyone in the family."

Gina continues: "My husband is English and went to boarding school. As a result he is very neat and always puts his clothes away; folds them and puts them in the drawer. He's been quite anxious, stressed

I suppose at my untidiness. He almost gave up and thought "I can't change Gina".

When Angella came in it was like music to his ears. He was very supportive and helped me see that if I got on top of it then my children would learn from me. And we had fantastic decluttering sessions either with or without Angella. I didn't mind doing it on my own provided I had the time to do it. It's stressful if there isn't enough time. My eldest boy is ten. He is naturally tidy. My eight year old daughter is untidy and we set aside time each week to tidy their rooms. I noticed that when their rooms are tidy, desks are clear and they have the tools such as paper, pencils and scrapbooks, they enjoy being creative. Our five year old's room isn't yet as prepared as I'd like it to be.

It's still a journey; a work in progress. We have a garage full of stuff we just haven't got round to selling or donating. We have downsized and have moved from a bigger home to a smaller home which I don't mind as it makes it cozier for the family.

(Being decluttered) reduces our stress, it increases our creativity because of the tidy environment and tidy mind, and it increases our time because with less stuff life is simpler. We're happier. Especially when you have a family, it's that real balance between having the time for recreation to be able to go out and enjoy cycling or going to the beach, with a home that feels like a sanctuary or a haven. Angella has taught me how to make things a bit more beautiful."

Laura, Auckland

"I got Angella in as my office was a bombsite. For several years I worked for a number of law firms and I'd always had a secretary. I started to work from home and I set up some systems that I thought would work but I discovered in the first couple of years working from home that it wasn't the systems that weren't working, it was me. I have never enjoyed the admin side of my job and I thought I would manage it. I would do it for a couple of months, leave it for a couple of months then do it. It got a bit overwhelming so I left it for a while. I had done a lot of my work on the computer so I didn't need the files, it was just the paperwork that was piling up. It got to the point that I didn't want to go into my office. A friend of mine who had used Angella to declutter her house said she also did offices."

Angella remembers Laura's office: "Her office area had become incredibly chaotic because there were no systems in place. Laura is a busy professional who in effect has two businesses, plus a busy household to run with husband and two children. The problem she was experiencing in her office was that the two different businesses had no clear defined areas (so papers and files for each business would end up piled on top of each other) and the office was also being used as a storage area for hobbies and non-office related items such as gifts, wrapping paper and cards, photos and other miscellaneous items.

So the first thing we did was to create a plan for exactly what needed to be kept in the office, and how we would define the areas (with cupboards and filing cabinets) for each business. We moved most of the personal items out of the office except for those which were able to be stored comfortably on spare shelves in the office cupboard.

Filing trays became designated by specific business and task which effectively sorted the paper and made the whole filing process much quicker and easier. Her desk was completely cleared and we put back on it only what she needed for the day to day running of her businesses. We also designated an in-tray for any items which she needed to action on an immediate daily basis and this sits on her desk.

Laura now has workable systems that she's using, her office looks tidy and uncluttered and she knows exactly where everything is (so she's stopped overbuying paper and stationery items). Her two businesses are also easier to administer because they each have their own working and filing areas. And best of all, we worked on creating some new structures in her life which means she's no longer working evenings, and is able to enjoy family time with a clear conscience that there isn't something else she should be doing at the time."

Laura continued: "Two children's bedrooms have also been decluttered. That has been highly successful and is ongoing. But it showed them what worked and what didn't. Whereas I used to comb their bedrooms when they weren't there and throw out stuff they thought was really important, Angella created a space for the important stuff. The rest of the house was OK. We did have a half a day session in the kitchen and that was pretty good. I had systems, I just got untidy. So we just tidied up for three hours and it's gone well. I never had a problem with the rest of my house."

And finally

Decluttering isn't an end in itself. However it is a means of getting you somewhere. What we mean is that by decluttering your home you have the chance to make use of its full potential. And by having an agreeable and functioning space to live in you are not only more likely to be at peace with yourself but also rub along better with others who share your home.

But most importantly the process we have described in this book helps remove clutter from your head giving you space to think and live.

Declutter your home and you will be surprised at the numerous ways your life improves. Enjoy the journey and thank you for listening.

Conclusion

This is where you can now review:

1. Which ideas within this book are you going to implement?

_____

_____

_____

_____

_____

_____

2. How do you think you are going to approach the family to have them help with the process, and set up new habits together?

_____

_____

_____

_____

_____

_____

3. What are you most excited about when you think of how your
    home will be after you've decluttered?

    _____

    _____

    _____

    _____

    _____

    _____